teach®
yourself

golf

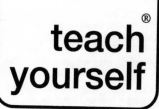

golf
david and patricia davies

For over 60 years, more than
50 million people have learnt over
750 subjects the **teach yourself**
way, with impressive results.

be where you want to be
with **teach yourself**

Illustrations by Barking Dog Art.

Every effort has been made to trace copyright for material used in this book. The authord and publishers would be happy to make arrangements with any holder of copyright whom it has not been possible to trace successfully by the time of going to press.

For UK order enquiries: please contact Bookpoint Ltd, 130 Milton Park, Abingdon, Oxon, OX14 4SB. Telephone: +44 (0) 1235 827720. Fax: +44 (0) 1235 400454. Lines are open 09.00–17.00, Monday to Saturday, with a 24-hour message answering service. Details about our titles and how to order are available at www.teachyourself.co.uk

For USA order enquiries: please contact McGraw-Hill Customer Services, PO Box 545, Blacklick, OH 43004-0545, USA. Telephone: 1-800-722-4726. Fax: 1-614-755-5645.

For Canada order enquiries: please contact McGraw-Hill Ryerson Ltd, 300 Water St, Whitby, Ontario L1N 9B6, Canada. Telephone: 905 430 5000. Fax: 905 430 5020.

Long renowned as the authoritative source for self-guided learning – with more than 50 million copies sold worldwide – the **teach yourself** series includes over 500 titles in the fields of languages, crafts, hobbies, business, computing and education.

British Library Cataloguing in Publication Data: a catalogue record for this title is available from the British Library.

Library of Congress Catalog Card Number: on file.

First published in UK 2006 by Hodder Education, 338 Euston Road, London, NW1 3BH.

First published in US 2006 by The McGraw-Hill Companies, Inc.

This edition published 2006.

The **teach yourself** name is a registered trade mark of Hodder Headline.

Typeset by Transet Limited, Coventry, England.
Printed in Great Britain for Hodder Education, a division of Hodder Headline, 338 Euston Road, London, NW1 3BH, by Cox & Wyman Ltd, Reading, Berkshire.

The publisher has used its best endeavours to ensure that the URLs for external websites referred to in this book are correct and active at the time of going to press. However, the publisher and the authors have no responsibility for the websites and can make no guarantee that a site will remain live or that the content will remain relevant, decent or appropriate.

Hodder Headline's policy is to use papers that are natural, renewable and recyclable products and made from wood grown in sustainable forests. The logging and manufacturing processes are expected to conform to the environmental regulations of the country of origin.

Impression number   10 9 8 7 6 5 4 3 2 1
Year   2010 2009 2008 2007 2006

contents

acknowledgements

The pros and other experts featured in this book have all given generously of their time and expertise but they are not responsible for what we've written or the way we've used the information. We hope that we've done them justice and that between us we've set you off down the fairway with hope in your heart and a smile on your face.

Numerous people have been involved in this project (some unwittingly) and their help has been invaluable.

We couldn't have done it without Maureen Madill, Patricia's sister, Advanced Fellow of the PGA, chief coach and confidence booster, who was unfailingly encouraging and kept us on track technically and we wouldn't have done it without the backing of the PGA, led by Sandy Jones, the chief executive.

Here follows an alphabetical list of everyone else (we hope) to whom we owe heartfelt thanks: Peter Alliss, Katie Archer, Eddie Birchenough, Luther Blacklock, Judith Blagg, Tony Blagg, Ann Blair, Nigel Blenkarne, Lynn Booth, Gillian Burrell, Bob Cantin, Tony Clayton, David Colclough, Tina Curley, John Cook, Paul Davies, Robert Davies, Sheila Davies, Simon Dicksee, Kitrina Douglas, Chris Duder, Peter Evans, Lawrence Farmer, Sally Farmer, Colin Farquharson, Richard Flint, Dermot Gilleece, Mike Gray, Emma Hadlow, John Jacobs, Peter Lane, Beverly Lewis, David Llewellyn, Peter McEvoy, Brian Mackie, Jimmy Madill, Peggy Madill, Lynn Marriott, Kate Marshall, Shirley Mason, Karl Morris, Charlie Mulqueen, Dave Musgrove, Pia Nilsson, Ian D. Rae, David Rickman, Victoria Roddam, Mike Round, Pat Ruddy, Andy Salmon, Lena Sellberg, Derek Simpson, Colm Smith,

Gillian Stewart, Nat Sylvester, Des Tobin, Peter Toogood, Bob Torrance, Jessie Valentine, Barry Ward, Keith Williams, Mark Wilson, Duncan Weir, Alison White, Lenny Woodhall and the team at Bodyzone in Walsall.

Finally, we would like to thank R&A Rules Limited and the USGA for granting us permission to reproduce sections of their etiquette text, ©R&A, USGA.

The game is what you make it and remember what Sir Henry Cotton, three times Open champion, said: Many golfers miss the greatest pleasure in the game – to play better – by not taking instruction. It is fun trying to do the right thing instead of hitting or missing all one's life. There are no natural golfers. We all have to be made.

The Professional Golfers' Association dates back to 1901 when three of the great professionals of the day J. H. Taylor, Harry Vardon and James Braid formed an organization to protect professionals' interests and promote the game of golf. It is now a flourishing association with 7,000 members. Most are club professionals specializing in the core subjects of coaching and retailing but increasing numbers are occupying managerial roles at clubs and resorts, at home and abroad, utilizing the skills of the PGA's modern training programme to broaden their career horizons.

The objectives of the PGA are:

1 To promote interest in the game of golf.
2 To protect and advance the mutual and trade interests of its members.
3 To arrange and hold meetings and tournaments for members.
4 To operate a benevolent fund for the relief of deserving members.
5 To assist members in obtaining employment.
6 To effect any other objects determined by the Association.

The Association plays a significant role at different levels, from junior coaching through to government level where it has an important role in helping to formulate and determine policy for the sport through its involvement in projects such as the Whole Sport Plan, Sport England and, most importantly, the implementation of a UK Coaching certificate in golf.

In recent times the PGA has restructured, notably in 1984 when the tournament playing division separated completely to form the PGA European Tour. The PGA retains close ties with the Tour and is a Ryder Cup partner, with an important position as the trustee of the actual Ryder Cup trophy donated by Sam Ryder. The PGA is dedicated to training and serving golf professionals, whose principal aim is to offer a highly professional service to amateur golfers at a club, driving range or other golf establishment.

Essex girl done good

It was the height of the swinging sixties and Beverly Lewis had just left school when, with her then boyfriend, now husband, Ken, she spotted a pitch and putt course in Billericay in Essex. Now, nearly 40 years later, she is the first woman ever to become captain of the Professional Golfers' Association. How did that happen? This is her account of that quite remarkable journey, from a junk shop in Southend to the rather more glorified confines of The Belfry, near Birmingham, the headquarters of the PGA.

'It was a freaky kind of thing, really,' she says. 'My family didn't play golf and I didn't do golf at school but Ken and I saw this pitch and putt and thought it might be fun, so we had a go. We quite enjoyed it and went back a few times but we always wondered why we didn't get one of those great big wooden clubs – all they gave us was a 7-iron and a putter. They said we didn't need a wood but we thought we did, so we went off to a junk shop and we both bought a driver, for about five bob (25p) each. We took them with us to the pitch and putt and off we went.

But that got us banned from the place. Halfway round there was a football pitch and Ken and I went off and hit balls to each other on it. When we got back, the starter asked us why we'd been so long, so we told him and he said, "I'm going to have you banned." Obviously we shouldn't have been on that pitch but we didn't know that at the time and as those were the days when you were scared of park-keepers, we never went back. Instead we found this nine-hole public course in Brentwood and decided to have a go on there.

I actually played my first round of golf in open-toed sandals. We said to them "Can we hire the clubs?" and they said we could and we asked "Can we hire the balls?" and they told us we would have to buy those. So we bought two each and we lost them all by the end of the second hole. Poor old Ken had to go all the way back to the shop and buy some more. And that was my introduction to golf.

I came in with no idea what it was all about, certainly with no expectations. The two of us just fell in love with it.

I played at three public courses all told before I ever joined a private club. Basildon golf club had just opened and was looking for new members, so we joined. We used to rush home from work, pick up some sandwiches my mother made, and off we'd go to the practice ground. We really didn't know whether we were any good or not but when I eventually had some lessons, the guy who was teaching me said "I think you should go in for the Essex championship." So I did, and I won it the first time I went in for it – because I didn't realize what it was all about. That was in 1972. I never won it again!

In the late 1970s there was a chance to get women's professional golf started and although I was never going to set the world of golf on fire I was happy to turn my lot in with them. I became the first chairman in 1978 and carried on from there.

But to be asked to be captain of the PGA, well, that was a total bolt from the blue. When Sandy Jones, the executive director, asked me in 2002, my response was, "Crikey, I can't believe what he's just said." I hesitated for all of three seconds before wanting to say yes but I didn't say yes for three weeks because I really didn't know what the job was.

I told Sandy I would need to talk to Ken first. Not a lot shocks him – but this did. He was just putting on a barbecue and I'd just got the potatoes on when I told him and he said, "I don't believe you." When it sank in, though, he said, "Of course you've got to do it. What an honour. What a great privilege. What a great thrill."

And he was right. It's been fabulous, absolutely fabulous. The image of golf is that it's for the rich, an elitist sport and it just is not. You know what Ken and I see all around us in golf? We see people having fun, so much fun, and that's what golf can be for everyone.'

Welcome to the game of a lifetime. It's fun, suitable for all the family, from toddlers to totterers, and you can play it on your own or with friends, for the exercise or for the competition, socially or seriously. It's endlessly adaptable and – a word of warning here – dangerously addictive.

It's that four letter word called golf, loathed with a passion by the good-walk-spoiled brigade but loved (and it has to be admitted sometimes detested) by its besotted, frequently frustrated devotees all over the world. It's played from Tahiti, where the dress code includes flip-flops, shorts and singlets to Tunbridge Wells, where a little more formality may be required; from Scotland, where it originated (though you may read that the Dutch started it all) to Van Diemen's Land; from the Gulf to the Himalayas; from sea to shining sea and all points in between. There are courses in Bhutan and Uzbekistan, Japan and Pakistan, Iran and the Caribbean. Golf is everywhere.

'Google' the word 'golf' and you get 27 million entries. The game can be played almost anywhere: on the moon, where Alan Shepard couldn't resist having a hit; below sea level at Furnace Creek in Death Valley, California, where the 18-hole course would be 218 feet under water were it not for the intervening mountains; at a height of 14,335 feet at the Tuctu club in Peru; 250 kilometres north of the Arctic Circle at Bjorkliden Arctic Golf Club, where you can play 24 hours a day during the summer. There is even a club 13 degrees north of the South Pole, the Scott Base Country Club, where players have to be kitted out in survival gear, which presumably restricts making a full turn on the backswing.

And exactly just what does that mean: a full turn on the backswing? We hope all will be explained in the pages that follow – or you could take a quick look at the glossary at the back of the book. Golf has a language of its own and we'll help you make sense of it. You'll read about great players, great deeds and great courses, most of which are also playable by mere mortals like ourselves.

You'll find that golf is for all shapes and sizes, that you do not have to be big or strong or fast or young or supple to play. You'll learn a bit about handicaps, rules and etiquette, about clubs, balls and course management and, with luck, you'll learn just why this game holds so many of us in its thrall.

Above all, you'll learn what it takes to play well and there will be practical tips and drills to help you. They'll stress the importance of sound fundamentals and purposeful practice so that you don't waste hours flailing away getting worse. A good teacher or coach is vital but a lot of new golfers think that they're not good enough to go to a professional and so they develop a load of bad habits before even thinking about signing up for lessons. Then they wonder why everything's suddenly so uncomfortable and their game is going backwards. Like so many of us they haven't thought to start at the beginning but just dived in somewhere in the middle and got in a muddle. Children are less likely to suffer from this affliction but the rest of us are not immune and our golf suffers.

Golfers who know learn from a pro, but if you can't – or won't – we'll bring the pro to you. The tips and advice in these pages come from some of the best coaches in the business, most of them members of the PGA and if you can't make a golfer of yourself with the aid of their expertise and ingenuity – and plenty of practice – then you're not really trying.

Of course, a lot depends on what you're trying to achieve. Golf caters to all degrees of enthusiasm: some people see it merely as a very attractive way of getting some gentle exercise, some as a way of relieving their competitive urges in an acceptable fashion. Some will want to learn just enough to be able to go to a golf club and get around the course without embarrassing themselves or their partners while others will want to learn the basics and then go on to see how good they can become. The great thing is that golf accommodates every level of ambition, whether you want to play socially (and sociably), to strive for a single-figure handicap, to become the local scratch man or even to turn professional. It's up to you.

Whatever your reasons for wanting to try golf, we want this book to take you anywhere – to give you the confidence not just to survive but to thrive in any golfing situation – and we hope that you'll take it everywhere.

Play well. Have fun.

(**NB** Throughout this book we have written the instructions for play for right-handed people. If you are a left-handed player, do remember to reverse the instructions when we talk about right and left.)

01

getting started

In this chapter you will learn:
- to set your own pace
- to start swinging
- to know no boundaries.

Tip at the top

Go with the flow.

Getting started is always the hard part of anything – sitting in front of a keyboard with a blank book in front of you is a prime example – but there comes a moment when you decide to take the plunge. Perhaps your friend says, 'Let's give this golf a go. It looks like it might be fun and it can't be that hard, after all the ball is just sitting there waiting to be hit and that old codger down the road plays every week, so we'll certainly be able to do it.'

Or perhaps your husband spends a lot of time on the golf course and you decide it's time for you to look into what the attraction is. Or perhaps you've seen it on television and are inspired to have a go. Or perhaps you've never heard of it, let alone seen it and a stranger comes to town and a whole new world opens up.

A word of warning before we begin: you are the key to all this. It's up to you how well you play golf. This book is a primer, a guide to the game, to set you off on the right track. It is not a step-by-step guide, although it should have a certain logic to it and give you an understanding of the basics. Words mean different things to different people and are open to misinterpretation, so you may find that we're saying much the same thing in different ways. We'll be trying to make ourselves clear but we won't always succeed. We'll be putting a lot of emphasis on keeping things simple, on concepts that are difficult to convey in words, vital things like feel, rhythm, balance and co-ordination. That's where you come in, trying things out, learning for yourself what a good shot feels like and what causes it, and what you're capable of comfortably.

A lot of people like to work with a ball from the off and that's no bad thing but there's lots of good work that can be done without the ball that will help you when you get out on the course. Ultimately, the approach you take will depend on your circumstances and your personal preferences. Most important is a willingness to learn and if you've bought the book – or been given it – that's a good indication that you've got all it takes to be a golfer.

What does a golfer look like?

Take a quick flick through the book and you'll see what golfers are like. Whoever you are, wherever you are, the chances are that there's already a golfer out there who looks like you, whatever your build. But no two swings are the same because no two people are the same – even twins develop differently. As Peter Lane, one of the professionals contributing to this book, puts it, 'Everyone has their own swing DNA and every golfer must understand that this is the timing that their body feels at ease with and can deliver results most times.'

John Jacobs, the doyen of coaches, one of the all-time great teachers, now in his eighties, has this tip: 'There is so much good golf on the television these days that I suggest you make a hero of someone and watch his or her rhythm, imitate the pace of their swing. Back in 1938, when I was 13, I saw Henry Cotton, who won three Opens and he became my hero. Every time I played after that I was Henry Cotton.'

Be careful to choose wisely. There's no use most of us trying to emulate Tiger Woods, the world's No. 1, for instance because we'd probably end up in the infirmary. Ernie Els, another of the world's top men, might be a better bet simply because his rhythm is much smoother and silkier. Many years ago, JoAnne Carner (née Gunderson), an American who gave the ball an almighty biff but was never the sweetest of swingers, said that she used to love playing matches against Angela Bonallack, an elegant Englishwoman, because her rhythm was so good that it was contagious.

The flip side is that watching someone with a rhythm that is the antithesis of your own is counterproductive. Jose Maria Olazabal and Nick Price are two men with very fast, whippy swing actions and John Daly would give you a hernia at the very least, so beginners beware. Beware, also, even when you become more experienced. You'll learn that it's better not to watch some people at all – or at least not closely – and not to use them as a template. One of the authors, who was then a lot better and a lot slimmer than he is now, played with a pro called Charlie Ward, a small, whippet-like man who swung very fast, and he started to do the same and began hitting the ball further. In time the extra distance went but the desire to swing quickly remained, to the detriment of his game. It was a rhythm that suited Ward to perfection but proved too much for lesser mortals.

Size doesn't matter

One great aspect of the game is that it caters to all shapes and sizes and the physiques of the top players in history have varied enormously. Jack Nicklaus, for instance, is only 5' 11" (1.8 m) and, at the latter end of his career, was 12 stones 8lbs (79.8 kg). But when he first emerged he was positively chubby, earning the nickname of 'Ohio Fats' (he came from Columbus, Ohio) and weighed in at nearer 16 stones (101.6 kg). At that time he hit the ball the furthest he ever did but he slimmed down – and let his hair grow out from the fierce crew cut he sported – for health and cosmetic reasons.

Then there is Woods, almost wraith-like in comparison to Nicklaus, given that he is the same weight but stands at 6' 2" (1.87 m). He is also immensely strong after spending long hours in the gym, exercising all the time with a view to strengthening the correct golfing muscles. Annika Sorenstam, the women's world No. 1, also works out ferociously but it is all carefully monitored and specific. Indiscriminate gym work can lead to a player getting muscle-bound and so getting in his own way, making a full swing next to impossible.

At the other end of the scale is the diminutive Welshman, Ian Woosnam, who is 5' 4½" (1.63 m) – that half inch (centimetre and a quarter) is very important! Woosie, as he is universally known, was, at the height of his career, one of the longest hitters in the game. This he achieved through a combination of strength, a great swing and wonderful timing; in the late 1980s and early 1990s he was so good that Severiano Ballesteros, the extravagantly talented Spaniard, said that Woosie had one of the best swings the game had ever seen.

As for the women, the two best English players of recent years have been Laura Davies and Alison Nicholas, who often played together in the Solheim Cup where they were invariably labelled 'little and large'. Both players won the US and British Women's Opens during their careers but Laura, at 5' 10" (1.77 m), was much, much taller than Alison, who was only 5' 0" (1.52 m) in her spikes. Different folks, different strokes but both outstanding golfers.

What you need

To play golf you need clubs (although just two will do to start with, one of which should be a putter) a ball (or balls) and somewhere to hit balls – this could be a field, a driving range or even off a mat into a net indoors.

Ian Woosnam – Raised in Shropshire, representing Wales, a Masters champion and captain of Europe in the Ryder Cup in 2006.

The ingenious and determined – and trick shot artists – will make do with what's to hand. A man called John Montague became a legend in America for being able to win playing with just a shovel – apparently – and not everyone starts with a club. In *A Woman's Way to Better Golf*, Peggy Kirk Bell, a super player who became a super teacher and who developed, with her husband and family, the Pine Needles Lodge and Country Club in Southern Pines, North Carolina, wrote about one of her best pupils: '...a 13-year-old whose family happens to live right next to our golf course. The parents don't play but she does. I first found her at the edge of the course hitting old balls using a thin piece of pipe. By watching many people play, she put together a natural swing. Now with golf clubs in her hands, she hits the ball about as far as I do.'

What we're doing

Golf is played from tee to green and ultimately the object of the exercise is to get the ball into the hole (cut in the green and marked by a flagstick) in the fewest number of shots. You do that by swinging the club so that you send the ball in the direction you want it to go: in other words you use the clubhead to propel the ball towards your target.

Gill's drills

Without a club

For our first bit of action (after warming up of course – don't neglect your stretches; you'll find a few warm-up exercises at the end of this chapter) we won't be using a club at all. Gillian Stewart, who used to star on the European women's tour (now called the LET – Ladies European Tour) alongside Davies and Nicholas and is now providing coaching in the Highlands of Scotland, at Fortrose and Rosemarkie, Muir of Ord and Aigas (you'd want to be a golfer just for the names), sets us in motion.

'You can train yourself to make the correct swing movements without a club. Position your feet slightly apart, place your hands together, palms facing, arms hanging loosely and swing them like a pendulum, first to the right and then to the left. If you think of the arc (or path) of your swing as a clock face, your hands start at six o'clock.

figure 1.1 (a) address position, palms together

(b) swing to the nine o'clock position, keeping the thumbs up

(c) swing through to three o'clock, keeping the thumbs up

To begin with make your swings from nine o'clock to three o'clock (or, if you play left-handed, from three o'clock to nine o'clock), keeping your head centred. [Note that you're not looking at the clock, you're looking out from it.]

You will find that your arms will rotate naturally as they cross the centre of your body. At nine o'clock your hands will be in a "thumbs up" position with your thumbs pointing directly upwards to the sky. This position is mirrored at three o'clock, with the thumbs up (see Figure 1.1 (a)–(c)). A good rule of thumb for this drill is: it's thumbs up to thumbs up.

It helps promote the feel of the body moving in sympathy with the arm swing. The shoulders will turn back and through and the weight will move in the direction that the arms are swung – to the right in the backswing and the left in the through swing.

With a club

You'll be able to do this same drill with a club in your hands – and you can take it on up to ten o'clock and two o'clock. There's no need to become obsessed with the exact time. It's a great exercise for helping you to swing *through* the ball and not *at* the ball.

Beginners often make the mistake of thinking that golf is purely a hitting game – in other words they hit at the ball instead of *swinging through* it. You must understand that it's not game over at impact, the swing doesn't stop when you hit the ball. The quickest way to make progress is to develop what I call a *swing mentality* where impact (connecting with the ball) is the by-product of the swing and not the target for the swing.

Clipping the tee

The next step is to introduce a feel of impact into your pendulum arm swing motion. This is best done by placing a tee peg in the ground at about three quarters of an inch in height (a couple of centimetres). The aim is to clip the tee peg out of the ground as you swing through. If you can start to clip the tee peg away consistently whilst keeping your action smooth, you are now ready to strike the golf ball.

Place a golf ball on top of the tee. The task is still the same: to clip the tee peg out of the ground. If you can mentally commit to this task, you'll find that you're striking the ball with the centre of the club face or in other words hitting the ball flush.

To sum up: these drills help you to swing through the ball. This is vital for the development of rhythm and balance. Remember, golf is a game primarily of movement, rhythm and balance.'

Far afield

Simon Dicksee is a man with a mission: he wants to introduce people to golf and give them the same pleasure and opportunities that he has enjoyed because of the game. He has worked all over the world, and his latest project is to bring girls from developing countries together in a golf and culture camp in Berlin. He describes himself as a 'freelance world golf developer' and he has been honoured by the Islamic Women Sport Federation for his work in Iran, where he has helped introduce many women and children to the game.

'Golf has no false barriers of colour, race, religion or politics and this message is opening doors into the education system,' Simon says. 'It is appreciated that it is not an elitist sport but one for everyone and, in particular, families. It's the perfect sport for women. There is one grass course in Tehran, which is 12 holes. It is in poor condition but very playable. There are four other courses, built on sand, in the south of Iran. The Iranians lack all forms of equipment and aids but they utilize anything they can. One of the great things, though, is that they have no preconceived ideas. Teaching people with no real concept of the game is a joy.

Working backwards from the hole

Like a lot of coaches I believe that you should start by mastering putting and then chipping. By starting with putting and moving on to chipping you soon learn all about clubhead control, swing path and speed. In this way we gradually build up the swing, with the player remaining comfortable and in control and keeping the essence of the game in mind, which is swinging at a target, with the ball only going in the direction that the clubhead is pointing.

Many golfers have never had the theory of clubhead speed explained to them in a simple way. Swing at the target and not the ball. Remember, the ball is *not* the target. If you *hit* at the ball, it creates tension in the muscles and decreases clubhead speed. If you focus on *swinging* at your target, you maintain the speed of the club through impact.

Another key to good contact, which leads to more distance, is keeping the swing simple in terms of its path and angle. Swing the club straight back, make a hinge and then up. This puts the club in a great position to deliver it square (flush, straight on) at impact and on to the finish. A swing with fewer movements is easier to repeat and much easier to time.

Great Dane

In my teaching career I have had many unlikely pupils but one in particular springs to mind because I feel he achieved an understanding of the innate simplicity of the swing. He was a chap from Denmark (where I lived and worked for 12 years) who sadly suffered from multiple sclerosis. His body had limited movement and his strength was waning. His mind was agile and his drive to learn, so that he could enjoy some quality time with his wife on the course, was immense. He had all the mental qualities that you require to achieve your goals. He had an acceptance of the limitations his body had. He had patience and a good sense of humour.

We worked on a method which enabled him to balance himself, grip the club and swing in such a way that he met the ball squarely to the target with his maximum clubhead speed. We also worked hard on his putting and short game, making that his strong area and we developed his understanding of how to score.

He achieved his goal of attaining a handicap and rounded the year off by winning a stableford competition. For me this story illustrates the essential for all golfers: understand your limitations, play to your strengths and use your mind.

Golf is a simple game that can sometimes be made difficult by the people who play it.'

Golf is everywhere

It's not beyond the bounds of possibility that Iran will produce a champion of its own one day because some of the most successful golfers have come from places that you would hardly suspect had heard of golf, let alone produced world-class players. For instance, there is a beach alongside a hidden estuary in northern Spain which is practically deserted, year round. Had you stumbled upon it 40 years ago you would have found a cherubic eight-year-old hitting balls he had 'found' on the nearby Pedrena course. Severiano Ballesteros had already fallen in love with the game and was learning the skills that would make him one of the most exciting players of all time.

Vijay Singh is the only world-class golfer so far to emerge from the Pacific islands, in his case Fiji. He lived on the main island of Viti Levu and the local course was at Nandi. This is a bone-hard, all but grassless area, with barely perceptible greens, with nothing at all attractive about either the course or the clubhouse, the latter just a shack where people congregated before going out. It needed an intense desire to play golf in those surroundings but Singh, an incredibly driven man, took himself all the way to the top of the world.

If you wanted to predict likely places for the emergence of world stars, you might think of Ayr, in Scotland, which has an Open Championship venue, Royal Troon, very close, plus dozens of other high-class courses. You almost certainly would not think of Ayr, in Queensland, a tiny town in the tropics devoted to the production of sugar. The main entertainment there is the cinema and that exists only because Karrie Webb, the golfing superstar who hails from the Australian Ayr, used some of her winnings to restore it after tropical damp had caused it to all but fall down.

Webb, who because of her success in reaching the world No. 1 spot became known as 'Cash-and-Karrie Webb' or – because she won wherever she went – 'World Wide Webb', is a classic case of being taught by the book. Kelvin Haller, her long-time coach and friend, who read voraciously and devoured every book and golf magazine that came his way, was confined to a wheelchair after an accident at work but it did not stop him teaching. He absorbed what the books had to say, passed on that knowledge to Webb and for many years remained her only coach. Pia Nilsson, a Swede with a holistic approach to coaching who has worked closely with Annika Sorenstam, well remembers the first time she set eyes on Webb: 'It was at the Ford Classic at Woburn and Sofia Gronberg [a Swedish professional] and I took one look at Karrie's swing, looked at each other and said, "Wow, who *is* this woman."'

The success of people like Ballesteros, Singh and Webb shows that if you have the determination and desire to succeed – and the talent – it doesn't matter where you come from. You can learn anywhere if you want to. It might not be on a course to begin with; it might be a driving range; it might be pitch and putt (in Ireland, for instance, many pitch and putters never bother with the big game at all). In Britain and Ireland you are rarely more than a few minutes away from a course or driving range – there are close on 3,500 golf facilities on the two islands, with England alone almost up to the 2,000 mark. There is almost bound to be something close to you and there are details of how to find them at the back of the book.

Age is only a number

Golf is a sport for all, which is something that the Scots, for instance, have always known and the best time to start is when you're ready. Little titches have started at 18 months and Tiger Woods is said to have played nine holes in 41 shots at the age of three but he was mad keen and imitating his father, so he was more than ready. There's no point forcing children to play if they don't want to, they'll let you know if they're interested. Many adults turn to the game when they have to give up sports that require too much running around or physical contact and the great thing about golf is that you can keep playing it for as long as the flesh and the spirit are willing – which can be a very long time. Arthur Thompson, a Canadian, once matched his age on his home course of Uplands, in British Columbia, (which measured more than 6,000 (5,486 m) yards in length). The remarkable thing was that he was 103 at the time. And George Evans, admittedly a retired professional, played Brokenhurst Manor, in Hampshire, 6,222 yards (5,689 m), par 70, in 71 at the age of 87. Not surprisingly, the 16 shots by which he bettered his age is believed to be a record.

Sweet spots

George Evans may have been long in the tooth but even at that advanced age and after a lifetime of hitting good shots, he would have remembered that mighty moment when, as a beginner, he first got a ball off the ground. He would have remembered, too, that magical moment when he first hit one so well that he hardly felt it – the eternal sign of near-perfection. Most people never forget that sweet split-second when club meets ball in exactly the right spot at exactly the right time and the ball soars into the sky on exactly the right trajectory for the first time.

If we can do it once, we can do it again and that's what keeps us coming back for more.

Gentle warm-ups

Lynn Booth, a physiotherapist who has done a lot of work with golfers, especially the top-notchers who play for England, stresses that the warm-up is no time to be trying to improve mobility. 'You should only be moving your joints and muscles through a range of movement that they are already capable of. Trying to improve mobility at this time will be counterproductive. You will often feel sore and the muscles may actually stiffen up, which is the opposite of what you hope to achieve.

Warm-up routines should be golf specific and you can practise the patterns of movement of the golf swing without the clubs prior to going to the practice ground.

The following exercises are important because they either enhance your cardiovascular system or take your body (muscles and joints) through movements that will be used during the golf swing or whilst walking on the course. (All the exercises are taken from the ELGA and EGU Physiotherapy Golf Exercises CD © 2005.)

- To raise the heart rate slightly try jogging on your toes or walking briskly to the practice ground or the first tee.
- Turn your head from side to side (cervical rotation).
- Tip your ear to your shoulder on both sides, keeping your chin facing forward (cervical side flexion).
- Arm circling (circle your arms in both directions).
- Brace your shoulders back (shoulder retraction).
- You should also move hamstrings, quadriceps and calves through a full range of movement.' (See Figure 1.2.)

Lynn also recommends trunk rotation, preferably in a sitting position, which can be done astride a chair, on a bench or, in due course, on an exercise ball. Hold a pole (or club) horizontally behind the upper back, just at or slightly below the level of the shoulders. Turn to the right, hold for a couple of seconds, then turn to the left and hold. Keep the knees pointing forward. Do ten repetitions, keeping the movement flowing.

Also try a pelvic tilt: stand with your shoulders and buttocks touching a wall and your feet a few centimetres away from the wall. Increase the hollow in the lower back, then flatten the hollow. Do not bend your knees.

figure 1.2 (a) hamstring stretch   **(b)** quadriceps stretch

(c) calf stretch

Before you start the trunk rotation and pelvic tilt, it is important to set your lower abdominals and your shoulder blades. To do the former, gently pull your tummy button in and up towards the spine but do not allow the pelvis to move. To set the shoulder blades, stand tall but relaxed, with your hands by your sides, palms facing your thighs and gently brace your shoulders back a few centimetres.

NB Remember that you should consult a doctor or other expert such as a qualified physiotherapist before undertaking any exercise routine, no matter how seemingly straightforward. Learn to do the exercises properly and they'll be a real benefit.

02

getting to grips

In this chapter you will learn:

- how to hold the club
- what GASP means
- about interlocking and overlapping.

Tip at the top

Good habits are the mainstay of good golfers.

We might as well start at the top here with the game's essentials as espoused by John Jacobs, who became known as 'Dr Golf' because of a great natural and nurtured ability to teach the game at all levels. If you wanted your game put on the right track, he was the man. 'I have spent most of my life,' he says, 'putting people in the correct position at address. That will not be the same address position for everybody but there will be one for everyone.' So it will do you no harm at all to use a Jacobs mnemonic to grasp the fundamentals of the starting position, from which the game flows. And it couldn't be easier to remember – GASP.

GASP simply stands for: *Grip*, *Aim*, *Stance*, *Posture*. In essence, the grip makes it possible to control the club face; how you aim the club face fixes the ball position and therefore the stance; correct posture makes it possible for a correct turn to be made and the swing to fall into place. That may not be completely clear to you just yet but it should all start to make sense as we progress.

Get a grip

There's no getting away from the importance of the grip. After all, it's what attaches you to the club, the implement without which you cannot play golf. It's vital. However, take it easy – there's no need to rush into it. Take time to feel it out and work it out. No coach disputes the importance of the grip but their approach to teaching it varies – and will vary again each time from player to player, depending on their physical attributes and requirements. Bear in mind that you're not in the business of throttling the club and that the golf swing is a fluid movement so you should hold the club sympathetically, without tension. That will allow you to use it most effectively. There are three different grips used in golf: the overlapping, or Vardon grip, the interlocking grip and the double-fisted grip.

Cook's creed

John Cook, a former winner of the Nigerian Open who is currently the national coach to Thailand and trains a number of county teams in Britain, stresses that you can make the game as easy or as hard as you want. Not surprisingly, he plumps for keeping it easy as the best and most enjoyable way to improve and he believes in letting you loose right away, reckoning to have you hitting balls into the air within 15 minutes. The grip is the first step.

For the purposes of this chapter we'll be calling the grip of the club the bit that you hold onto at the top of the shaft, the handle, to try and avoid confusion. Also, long-suffering lefties please reverse the instructions: your top hand is your right hand, it's the other way round for right-handers. Now over to Mr Cook.

'I start by putting a golf club in your hand – a 7-iron is favourite. Grip the club by shaking hands with the handle with your left hand [making sure the handle is lying along the bottom of the fingers, not in the palm]. The thumb of your left hand should now be on top of the handle, slightly right of centre. The back of your left hand should be pointing the same way as the club face – towards your target. Now, with the clubhead resting on the ground and aiming at the target, you should be able to look down at the back of your left hand and see two knuckles. The top of the handle should be protruding out above your left hand by about half an inch.

Now put your right hand onto the grip in such a way that it is parallel to the left – palms facing, in effect – with the handle fitting into the fingers of the right hand. Fold your right hand over so that your left thumb fits snugly into the lifeline of your right hand. The little finger of the right hand should just overlap the index finger (also called the forefinger) of the left hand, making sure that the hands are one unit and will work in concert. This is probably the most complicated part of the entire swing but I consider it probably the most important.'

The overlapping grip

The grip described above is the overlapping or Vardon grip (see Figures 2.1 and 2.4). It could be called golf's grip of choice. The vast majority of the world's golfers use it and it is named after Harry Vardon who popularized its use in the late nineteenth, early twentieth century. Vardon has been almost completely forgotten these days but he still holds the record for the number of Open wins (six) and as he won a US Open as well, has more majors to his name than any other British golfer. He ranks alongside Sam Snead and Arnold Palmer in the matter of majors won, one ahead of Nick Faldo and Lee Trevino. Bernard Darwin, the distinguished first golf correspondent of *The Times*, wrote, 'I do not think that anyone who saw Vardon in his prime will disagree as to this: that a greater golfing genius is inconceivable.'

The Vardon grip, as has been graphically described, features the little finger of the right hand wrapped over the index finger of the left and is said to neutralize, in a right-handed golfer, the greater power of that right hand and prevent it from taking over.

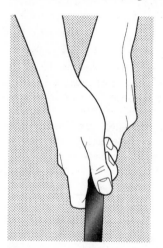
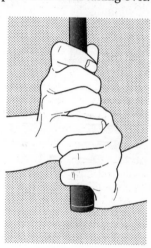

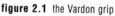
figure 2.1 the Vardon grip

The interlocking grip

For most players the Vardon grip is the best option but it is a strange and incontrovertible fact that the two best golfers ever to play the game, Jack Nicklaus and Tiger Woods, have opted not to use it. They employ what is called the interlocking grip. This simply means that instead of the fingers overlapping each other, they are intertwined (see Figure 2.2).

Both these giants of the game have their reasons for using a grip said to get the hands working even more closely together than the Vardon. In Nicklaus's case it is because he has, for a relatively big man, very small hands and he feels he needs to anchor them together as closely as possible. For Woods it is a relic of the days when he first started – at about the age of 18 months. Obviously he had the smallest of hands at that time and needed all the grip he could get just to hang on to the club. As he has never stopped winning from that day to this he has never felt the need for change.

Colin Montgomerie, Europe's best golfer for many years, winner of the Volvo Order of Merit eight times, including seven in succession from 1993 to 1999, then again in 2005, also adheres to the interlocking grip. 'I've got quite big hands,' admits Monty, 'but the fingers just sort of slipped together when I was ten and have stayed there ever since.' And Sandy Lyle, on a whim, decided to change from overlapping to interlocking in the course of winning the Lancome Trophy in 1984.

figure 2.2 the interlocking grip

The double-fisted grip

The third common grip used in golf is the two-handed, double-fisted or baseball grip (although strictly speaking a baseball grip has the hands further apart) (see Figure 2.3). It's not a bad way to start, being the natural thing to do when first picking up a club. Kids often also have the left hand below the right (also cross-handed or cack-handed) but that's nothing to worry about early on – just leave them to it. John Gallagher, a Scot who reached the final of the Amateur Championship in 2005, defied orthodoxy with his cack-handed grip but most players, as they learn more about the game, find one of the other two grips more consistent. The main weakness of the two-handed grip is that the hands have a tendency to act independently of one another, to the detriment of the swing. However, if you bear in mind that the hands should work as one unit, you may find that it suits you.

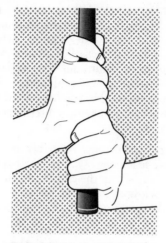

figure 2.3 the double-fisted grip

Harvey Penick, the legendary teacher from Texas, whose distilled wisdom first appeared in *Harvey Penick's Little Red Book*, a joy and a delight that is full of good sense, reckoned that 'the best thing to do is to find a grip that fits you and feels good and then stay with it'. He also had a little self-deprecatory word of warning about getting too complicated: 'I can go on and on talking about the grip until it gets too deep for me to understand.'

Hang loose

All this talk of interlocking, overlapping and Vardon might have you a bit baffled, so take a breather by listening to Eddie Birchenough, the pro at Royal Lytham and St Annes, a man of great experience and nous.

'Too much lip service is paid to the grip,' Eddie contends. 'All you are doing is attaching yourself to the club, that's the only function of the grip and I want my pupils to first of all get some movement, some motion, with the club in their hands before working on a formal grip. If you start by concentrating exclusively on the grip and don't pay attention to the body positions, then it won't work. I think the beginner can be stifled at the start with too much concentration on the grip. It's inevitable that there will be too much tension in the hands and that will affect the rest of the swing.

The grip is a highly individual thing, just as people are very different individuals. There are people with long fingers, stubby fingers – really it's all about finding what people are comfortable with. I taught Russell Claydon, who had a long career on the European Tour and he overlapped with two fingers because his were so fat and podgy that he couldn't interlock with any comfort. He tried the Vardon grip once for half an hour and finished by saying it was hopeless, he couldn't feel the clubhead at all.

Of course different age groups probably need to be treated differently. If I were teaching, say, a ten-year old child, I would ask him or her to just pick up the club – and they'd probably do so with left hand below right – and then just swing it, so that their instinctive side comes out. There's time to move the hands around later.

An older person, or pensioner, coming to the game for the first time, might be better off with a double-handed grip, and if I got a retired sportsperson, say a cricketer with good hand-eye co-ordination but no experience of golf, I'd ask him to just hit the golf ball for as many fours or sixes through mid-wicket as possible.

Of course the grip is important but not so much at the start of a golfer's career. It can always be adjusted to suit the person once some idea of the swing has been absorbed.'

Eddie's easy grip tip

Eddie suggests that to acquire a conventional Vardon grip, it is worth buying a 'reminder' grip, one of those moulded grips that encourages the hands and fingers into the correct position. You can practise this in front of the tv and just grip and re-grip until it feels natural.

Gene Sarazen, who won the Open in 1932 and holed in one in the 1973 Open at the age of 71, made a lovely crack about Sam Snead, the smoothest swinging of champions: 'Sam still thinks that the Vardon grip is a suitcase.'

figure 2.4 side-on view of the Vardon grip

figure 2.5 the trigger finger

More practicalities

Nigel Blenkarne, a man of many parts, about which more later, has been a PGA pro for more than 30 years and he has a useful little tip on how to get the club into the correct part of the top hand – the left hand for a right-hander, the right hand for a left-hander.

'It's important that the club should fall into the base of the fingers, with the back of the top hand facing your target and a simple way to feel this is to take hold of the wire handle of a driving range ball basket [as an aspiring golfer you will become familiar with these]. Doing this naturally you will pick it up with the wire handle falling into the middle joints of the fingers. Try it and see how it feels and hold your golf club in a similar way.'

Here are four simple points to bear in mind about the grip:

1 The palms should be roughly facing each other.
2 The club should be in the fingers (as opposed to across the palm). This is important for flexibility of the wrists.
3 The left thumb needs to be slightly right of the centre of the handle. This is particularly important because at the top of the swing it will be underneath the club, supporting it and keeping you in control.

4 The right forefinger should be crooked around the handle as though pulling a trigger. Position the right thumb on the handle pointing slightly to the left. This also helps aid stability and control.

Most important of all: Make sure the club face is aiming squarely at your target throughout this process.

Grip pressure

How tightly should you hold the club? This is an important question and Gillian Stewart gives her take on the subject.

'The correct grip pressure allows you to feel the weight and the position of the clubhead throughout the swing and keeps you in touch with what you're doing. It's vital for developing a rhythmical movement. Too loose and the club moves in your hands; too tight and the tension is swing-wrecking: holding on like grim death is a no-no. One of the best analogies I've heard for the correct grip pressure was attributed to the American teacher Bob Toski, who likened it to holding a small bird in your hands: if your grip is too loose, the bird escapes, if it's too tight, the bird is crushed.

If you take one as being as light as possible and ten as being a grip like a vice, try aiming for a grip pressure of three to four.'

Figure of eight

This is a great little exercise for teaching yourself about the hands and the clubhead. Maureen Madill, an Advanced Fellow of the PGA, suggests:

'Take your grip and, holding the club straight out in front of you, inscribe a figure of eight in the air. Make sure you use your hands rather than your arms and you'll start to understand what you're trying to do. A free and easy flexibility of the wrists is important and stops you having too much tension in your forearms: firm hands, soft (relaxed) arms, that's the combination we're seeking.'

Gloves

It's entirely up to you whether you wear a glove or not. Most players wear one on their leading hand, the one that goes onto the club first; some players wear two; some wear none. It's up to you. See what suits you. There's a wide selection to choose from. But if you do wear a glove, make sure it fits you. And buy more than one at a time, so that you can reduce the wear and tear.

Stay balanced

Here's an exercise that will improve your balance and core stability but be careful when you start practising it because you'll wobble all over the place at first. Stand on one leg with the other leg raised in front of you so that the thigh is parallel to the ground. Close your eyes and stay balanced for as long as you can without holding on to anything. You'll probably manage only a few seconds at first but some people practise it when they're cleaning their teeth. It's not that easy and you don't want to go crashing into basins, baths or toilets and do yourself serious damage so approach with care and keep your eyes open to begin with. (Further warning: it will probably make you laugh but if you persevere, it should improve your golf.)

03

aim, stance, posture and swing

In this chapter you will learn:

- how to aim
- how to stand
- how to start swinging.

Tip at the top

All good swings flow from a good stance.

This chapter is a continuation of GASP – grip, aim, stance, posture. In other words we are looking at the set-up – the base from which your swing starts. If you get this right, you're on your way to playing good golf.

The tip at the top comes from Davis Love III's father, also Davis Love, and a very good player and even more gifted teacher. His son became a very successful tournament professional, renowned for his long hitting and won the US PGA Championship in 1997. You'll find that styles change but the eternal verities remain and in golf what you're trying to do every time is strike the ball solidly in the direction in which you're aiming. Setting up correctly gives you every chance of doing just that. The correct address position, as your stance – how you stand to the ball, how you set up – is also known, introduces you to the art of the possible.

Aim

You've taken your grip on the club and the first thing to check is that the club face is square, not angled to the left or the right. Here's a simple tip to check that you've got it right: lift the club up out in front of you, arms extended and check that the leading edge of the sole (the bit that sits on the ground) of the club is vertical (see Figure 3.1). When it is, you're on course.

figure 3.1 check that the leading edge is vertical

Parallel universe

Now, standing behind the ball, look at the ball, look at your target and imagine a line between the two. This imaginary ball-to-target line is a vital line – think of it as a lifeline to good golf – and is the one to refer to constantly as you prepare yourself to hit a shot. That's where you want the ball to go, so that's how you set yourself up. It's the key to getting yourself aligned correctly. The club face is positioned squarely – at right angles – to this imaginary line and you then settle yourself into golf's version of a parallel universe.

Imagine another line that runs parallel to the ball-to-target line and align your body along it. As a general rule your shoulders, hips, knees and toes should be parallel to this second line. A classic image is to visualize yourself setting up on a railway line, with the ball and club face on one track and you on the other (Figure 3.2).

figure 3.2 imagine that you are lining up on a railway track

You can use one or two clubs laid on the ground to check that you've got this right and are lining up correctly. Take your time. This is worth getting right (see Figure 3.3).

figure 3.3 lay a club on the ground to help you line up

A common misconception is that the shoulders point towards the target but always bear in mind: it's the club face that points at the target. If you still have to be convinced, try aiming the club face at the target and aiming the shoulders at the same target. Makes you feel all bitter and twisted, doesn't it? Unwind, relax. Think parallel universe, think railway lines, think keeping on track, think whatever it takes to encourage you to point yourself and your club face in the right direction, the place where you want the ball to go.

Aim like Annika

Annika Sorenstam may be the best woman golfer in the world with a game that is light years away from what most of us can aspire to but it doesn't mean that we can't learn from her. In her excellent book *Golf Annika's Way*, she addresses the importance of aligning your shoulders properly and recommends checking the position of your forearms to check on your shoulders. It's difficult for you to see where your own shoulders are but your arms are out there in front of you and Annika has a look at the front of her forearms to see that she's on the right track.

She suggests getting someone to hold a club against the top of your forearms to help ensure that you're all matched up from top to toe.

Extra eyes

This is a good time to reiterate the importance to a golfer of another pair of eyes, preferably a trained and discerning pair like those of Annika's coach Henri Reis, who has been helping her since her schooldays. You may be able to teach yourself but you can't watch yourself. That's why even the best players need a coach, a teacher, an educated observer to keep them on the right lines.

Aiming tip

To make things easier on the golf course, you can also get into the habit of having a target closer to you, to help you set the ball off on the right line. Say you're aiming at the flagstick (which won't always be the case) a couple of hundred yards away, it helps to pick a spot three or four feet ahead of you that is on your line and to use that as your aim finder. It could be a particular bit of grass, a divot, a daisy, anything.

Jack Nicklaus first did this in the 1970 Open at St Andrews. As he explained in his autobiography *My Story*: 'The Old Course is the hardest I know on which to align yourself correctly for both drives and approach shots. Its legendary undulations make the majority of its landing areas invisible as the ball is addressed and there are no trees and relatively few other landmarks to serve as guideposts. Correctly targeting myself was tough...until one of the guys I was playing with happened to mention the concept of using a short marker as an aiming aid. "Gee," I said to myself, "it's obviously a darn sight easier to align yourself on a spot a few feet ahead of the ball than on something a couple of hundred yards away. What a great idea!" ...This system...helped enormously not only in that championship but for the rest of my career.'

Stance and posture

Put simply this just means how you stand to the ball. The *Chambers Dictionary* definition of stance includes this: 'a posture adopted in standing; the standing position of someone about to play the ball in golf...'

Its definition of posture includes the following: 'the way one holds one's body in standing...; a particular position or attitude of the body...'

Stance and posture may not be exactly the same thing but in golf they are indivisible and if you get them right, you're giving yourself every chance of playing decent golf.

Keith Williams, a PGA Master Professional (there is no higher accolade), is in no doubt that: 'Posture is the key to everything. Good posture is not a static position but allows you to feel balanced and prepared. You should feel dynamic and ready to begin the swing action. Good posture makes it easier to turn the hips and shoulders and swing the arms and club on the right path throughout the swing. It also allows you to remain balanced throughout the swing.

Flex your knees slightly, to allow the upper body to lean gently forward from the hips and keep your weight evenly balanced – both between the right and left foot and between the heel and the ball of each foot. Think of your head as a relaxed extension of the spine, keeping your chin in a comfortable position, neither tucked into your chest nor jutting high into the air. You're ready for action.'

This little rhyme may help you with the basic position (see Figure 3.4):

Stand to attention
Stand at ease
Bend from the hips
Flex the knees.

Experiment. Shift your weight around and test out how it feels. Communicate with your feet. See what happens when you move your weight onto your toes; back onto your heels; too far to the right; too far to the left. As with most things finding the right balance makes life a lot easier.

figure 3.4 (a) stand to attention

(b) stand at ease

(c) bend from the hips

(d) flex the knees

Take a look at good players and study their posture and have a good look at the illustrations here to see what's required, although bear in mind that they are guides only. As Keith Williams says: 'Posture is one area where a picture speaks a thousand words.'

figure 3.5 good posture will help your golf

figure 3.6 use a club to check your posture

Guidelines

A useful way to check that your back is straight and in its natural alignment is to hold your club along your spine, with the grip at the base of your spine and the head at the top (see Figure 3.6). You can use a mirror or a window to check your reflection.

Another exercise to help you find the right position is to grip the club, stand with your feet about shoulder-width apart, your knees slightly flexed and hold your arms out in front of you at roughly shoulder height. Slowly lower the club to the ground, bending slightly from the hips and keeping your back straight. The clubhead should be resting on the ground opposite a point that's midway between the centre of your feet and your front foot (that is the foot nearer the target). Your arms are hanging loosely from the shoulders and your hands will be more or less in line with your nose and mouth. (This is not something to be obsessive about, it's just an aid to check that you're in the right position.) Your left shoulder (if you're playing right-handed) will be higher than your right, which is logical because your left hand is higher up on the club than your right hand. One last point, the distance you stand from the ball will be dictated by the length of the club you're using, so if you set up carefully and well, how far you stand from the ball will take care of itself.

Point to note

We're still using a 6-or 7-iron for this – a mid-iron – and the ball position (essentially where the clubhead is) will change depending on which clubs you are using. As a rough guide, it will be in the centre of your stance with short irons and just inside the left heel with the driver. Just remember that ball position varies depending on what club you're using: it is not set in stone.

In his book *50 Years of Golfing Wisdom*, John Jacobs is quite candid about the importance of the set-up: 'It really is absurd for an intelligent person to make no effort to get things right from the start. Yet most golfers don't...The set-up of a shot can be learnt consciously and without any great mental or physical effort. With a little care and application, any one of us can set up a good swing. Make the effort – and a good swing becomes a probability rather than an impossibility.'

Get set and start swinging

Nigel Blenkarne once did an instructional series for a newspaper with Mike Catt, the former England rugby international and they worked hard to give Mike a consistent pre-shot routine.

Nigel recalls: 'Mike used to walk up to the ball and plant his feet in position first and then put the club behind the ball and the *last* thing he did was position his hands on the club. Also, because he was used to playing a fast-moving ball game the whole process, from planting his feet to starting the swing, took about three seconds. Sometimes he got the distance he was standing from the ball correct but more often than not he was inconsistent and the results were erratic.

How we improved this was by making sure that taking hold of the club correctly became the *first* stage in the set-up. This should be done well before going near the ball and at first you may want to ground the club to take your grip. Later you may prefer doing it in mid-air but check that the club face is square when you take your grip.

Then step forward to the ball with your feet close together and your back foot (the right one if you're right-handed) closer to the ball-to-target line than your other foot. This makes it easier to aim the club face at the target. When you're placing the club behind the ball, aiming squarely at the target, ensure that you tilt forward from the hips with your spine at the correct angle. Then the final adjustment is to bring each foot into the position you want for the stance (see Figure 3.7). Spend a few seconds fine tuning this by shifting your weight from one foot to the other until you feel absolutely comfortable. Combine this with a small and gentle waggle of the club, just lift the clubhead off the ground an inch or so and flex your hands and wrists so that the clubhead moves back a few inches and then return it to the ball while settling your feet. This helps prevent tension in the set-up.

This whole process now takes Mike about 10–12 seconds instead of three. He hits a far higher number of good shots, takes fewer shots per round and gets round quicker. It's worth taking a few seconds longer setting up to each shot correctly.'

Nigel's swinging drill

Nigel also has a good drill to help you with your footwork and weight transfer as you swing. He suggests: 'Take hold of a club and hold the shaft horizontal, resting in your fingers, with your

figure 3.7 (a) setting your grip

(b) aiming the club face and setting your feet

(c) address position

thumbs pointing in towards you and your hands spaced apart about the width of your hips. (Using a longer club will give you a better sensation of how your body should turn in the golf swing.)

Taking your usual stance and bend forward posture – use your thumbs and the club shaft as a reference point – make the backswing hip turn of approximately 45 degrees, keeping the sole of your back foot flat on the ground. Most of your weight will be on this back foot now. (A slight lift of the heel of your front foot – about an inch – is OK.)

To change direction, your front hip should be pushed back as the back foot rolls onto its instep (the inside of the foot) and your back knee and hip move forward to finish level with the front knee and hip. At this point your back foot should be on its toe pointing directly upwards. Most of your weight is now on the outside edge of your front foot and your navel is facing towards your target.

This drill is very simple and effective to do indoors or outdoors before play or practice. Just remember one simple thought: your weight must move in the same direction as your arms, back on the backswing and forward on the forward swing.'

And never forget that at its most basic the golf swing is two turns with a swish in the middle.

Cook's turn

John Cook, who likes to have his first-timers hitting the ball into the air in 15 minutes, uses this simple drill to give you the feeling of the correct body movement in the swing. 'Whilst in your set-up position, slide the golf club across your back and put your arms over the club so that the shaft fits through the crook of your elbows, with the grip end facing the target. Turn your body until the grip faces the ball, now turn back until the clubhead goes past the ball. It's a simple movement and is the exact movement the body makes during the swing. Keep practising it and use it to loosen up before you play.

Now all we have to do is put arms onto the body movement. Swing the club back by turning the same way as you did in the drill, only this time you are holding the club properly. Make sure that the thumb of your left hand is directly under the shaft at the top of the backswing (if you get your grip right to begin with, that'll be no problem). The shaft of the club will now be pointing parallel to your target line. Now swing the club back down with the same body movement as you used in your drill. At the completion of your follow-through, the thumb on your left hand should be directly under the shaft again. Try to feel that the ball gets in the way of your practice swing and it will go up in the air and forward.'

Balanced individuals

We'll leave the last word here to Gillian Stewart, who stresses the importance of *balance* throughout the swing. 'In order to swing in balance we have to start in balance. Make sure your weight is 50–50 between your left foot and your right. Your weight should be right in the centre of your feet – neither on your heels or your toes – and a good way to get a sense of this is to rock back and forwards from your toes to your heels.

Somewhere in the middle you will feel your balance point. Here's a good piece of mental imagery to have when you are getting set up to the ball and focusing on your balance: imagine you are in a darkened room and there is someone in that room who is going to try and push you over. Your challenge is to stay upright but you don't know from which side they'll come at you. How would you hold yourself? You'd definitely want your weight to be centred to resist the push. If you were back on your heels or on your toes, you'd definitely be a pushover.

Finishing in balance is important too, so here's a post-swing drill to practise. You've hit the ball, it's in the air and you've just completed your follow-through: hold it. Hold this pose until the ball stops rolling. If you can hold your follow-through like this, you are in balance. It is a vital part of swing imagery. I often tell people to imagine that they are getting their photograph taken at the end of their swing, so they have to hold their position. It helps achieve a consistently balanced finish, which usually means quality ball-striking.

If you start in balance and finish in balance, it's more than likely that you'll be swinging in balance. When you do that, it feels smooth, relaxed and effortless.'

Retief Goosen (balance) – A firm left side has helped the South African maintain perfect balance.

A swing drill

John Jacobs says that 'the club must travel from the inside on the downswing to the inside again after impact' and Derek Simpson, the senior teaching professional at The Belfry, has just the drill to help you achieve that. 'Place four shoe boxes on the ground as shown, put the ball in the middle and hit it without hitting the boxes.' If you're not a shoeaholic like Imelda Marcos, use something else, for example headcovers.

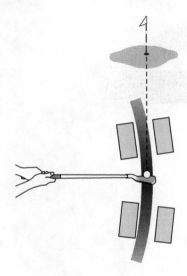

figure 3.8 a useful swing drill

04

putting

In this chapter you will learn:
- how to hole out
- how to develop feel
- what good putters do.

Tip at the top

Every putt is straight.

The putting green is where a lot of people start learning the game and the great Harvey Penick was an advocate of starting at the hole and working backwards towards the tee. In his classic *Little Red Book* he said that he liked to see youngsters working on and around the practice green with a putter, a chipping club and one ball. They learn to score by chipping towards the hole, taking their putter and holing out. It teaches them feel – and Penick stressed that 'a chipping stroke is just a short version of a full swing' – and that there are no second chances out on the course. It was, he admitted, more difficult to persuade adults that this was the way to begin their golfing careers.

A few basics

Place the ball six inches (15 cm) from the hole, then use the putter to hit the ball into the hole. Once you've done that easily enough, move the ball 12 inches (30 cm) from the hole and hole out again. Then move back to 18 inches (45 cm), two feet (60 cm) and so on. Get comfortable holing putts.

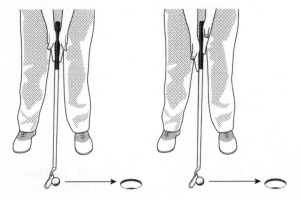

figure 4.1 position of the hands when putting

How do you grip the club? Well, that's up to you, bearing in mind that your sole aim is to use the putter head to propel the ball into the hole. A simple way to start is to have your palms facing each other, then clap them onto the handle of the putter, slide one hand down a bit and close your fingers around the handle (grip) with your thumbs pointing down the centre of the shaft. The blade of the putter should be square, with the leading edge at right angles to the imaginary ball-to-target line. In other words, aim the putter at your target (see Figure 4.1).

Have your toes, knees, hips and shoulders parallel to the imaginary ball-to-target line and the eyes, ideally, over that line. Stances will vary but the shoulders should certainly be parallel to this line and that's easiest if everything else is aligned similarly. You should keep everything below the waist nice and still. Try this without a putter, clapping your hands together then swinging your arms and shoulders, with your lower body steady (see Figure 4.2).

To get a feel for longer putts, roll a ball towards the hole as though you were playing bowls. You can use a tennis ball or a golf ball for this, just use it to get a feel for distance. You can do this at home too, using a coin, a glass, a chair leg, or almost anything as your target.

Here's a simple drill from Derek Simpson, who coaches at The Belfry, which should help make the hole look bigger: 'You can practise this on the carpet at home or in the office. Putt towards a coin, trying to make the ball finish on the coin. After practising this for a while, the hole looks huge.'

figure 4.2 practise without a ball, swinging your arms and shoulders but keeping your lower body steady

Different game

Putting is often referred to as a game within a game and while it certainly is that, requiring totally different techniques and disciplines, it is also a vital component of the overall game itself. How well you putt will often determine how well you score or will turn what could have been a catastrophic round into something on the fringe of respectability. Equally, bad putting can be a thing of enormous frustration if the rest of the game is going well and given that golf sometimes seems to mirror life, all too often you will play well and putt badly or putt well and play badly. It is a very rare thing, though, for the top professionals to have a low score unless they putt well. If they hit shots close to the pin and hole the putt, they call it 'converting' their chances.

Beginners and inexperienced golfers often putt well simply because they expect to. They have no baggage, no long history of missing crucial putts at critical times. In general what makes putting difficult is the mental aspect that comes into play the longer you have been playing. It is one thing to tap a ball casually into the hole from three feet when the match is already lost or your score does not matter but quite another thing when that putt is to win the match, the money and the gloating rights or to break 100, 90, 80 or whatever the target is for the first time. When you're playing for a good score, every putt counts. It is not the slightest use saying after a round that if you hadn't three-putted four times, you would have broken 100 or whatever. Your score is what it is and every putt counts.

No problem

Putting, to those who do not play golf, looks simple and it is – physically. It makes no onerous demands on the physique – anyone can knock a ball along the ground with a flat-faced stick towards a hole in the ground – and theoretically there is no reason on earth why all putting should not be accomplished successfully. The object of the entire game is to get the ball in the hole in the fewest number of strokes and, usually, you will finish off with your putter. There are almost as many ways of going about putting as there are people playing the game. It is the one part of golf that can be completely individualistic and, if it works for you, then it is acceptable. Having said that, most of the top players will incorporate certain basic principles in their stroke, some of which you'll pick up here.

Alliss

Peter Alliss is one of the most famous names and certainly the most recognizable voice, in world golf. He has been television's best commentator for so long that there are generations of players and viewers who do not know what a fine player he was in the 1950s and 1960s, winning championships and playing in Ryder Cups. Peter, like his father Percy, who was also a Ryder Cup player, had a wonderful swing and allied immense power to what was in his youth a delicate and successful putting stroke.

'When I was in my teens,' he recalled in his classic book *Alliss Through The Looking Glass*, 'I was a wonderful putter. I felt I could knock everything into the hole and I couldn't get it on to the green fast enough.'

In those days, putting was a simple matter for Alliss, who later suffered so much on the greens that he acquired the car registration PUT 3 and it adorns his Bentley to this day. He says, 'I have learned two things above all about putting: every putt is a straight putt and in putting you hit the ball and nothing else.'

The great man, a former captain of the PGA, explains that once you have decided on the line of a putt, you just hit it straight, directly along the line you have seen. The contours of the green, the slope of the ground, the thickness of the grass, the dampness or dryness of it, are all influences but all you can do, and should do, is have faith in your own judgement and hit the ball straight along the line on which you have decided. Alliss is not an advocate of brushing the grass with the sole of the putter, which he describes as 'a dangerous distraction'. His advice is: 'Forget it. Don't complicate your thinking on putting. Make it as simple as possible.'

He adds: 'The stance should be comfortable and the grip should be comfortable. That's all. You have nothing further to worry about concerning stance and grip. You hold the putter firmly enough to be aware of a little tension in the separate fingers, but just keep the whole operation as simple as possible.'

Alliss also has a good tip for those very long putts that look so difficult when the pin is just a blur 50 feet (15 m) or more away. 'Try not to hole them,' is his somewhat startling advice. 'Try to get them inside a target circle of about two feet around the hole. That will mean your next putt is safe – and you will be surprised how many go in when you are not trying to hole them.'

Faxon

The insistence on keeping it simple is the best possible advice and it is echoed by Brad Faxon, a player considered to be the finest putter on the US tour, consistently finishing with the lowest average number of putts per round over a season. The American sounds uncannily like the Alliss of the 1960s when he talks about putting.

'Don't think about it too much,' Faxon says. 'Look at the line and trust your first instinct. You can't be good at putting with too much conscious thought.'

Another Faxon adage is: 'Do not be afraid to miss.' He stresses: 'Worrying gets you into trouble and ties you up in knots.'

That's all well and simple, easy to say but more difficult to put into practice and Faxon has some sound practical advice:

'You need a good putter, a good stroke and a good attitude and of these attitude is the most important. There's never been a great putter who didn't have a great attitude. Putting is like anything else that is great in sport: you have to believe in yourself and you have to practise. It irritates me when people think I'm a natural and don't have to practise. I practise and practise and practise. Putting should be the easiest thing to improve because it requires the least amount of physical talent.

On every green I check out the wind, the break, whether the putt is uphill or downhill, if the green is firm or soft – but I don't take a lot of time doing that. I pick out a line and aim the ball at it.

Before I start a round I take a pen and draw a line on the ball about an inch and a half long. After I have decided on the line of my putt, I put the ball down with that line pointing in the direction I want to hit the ball.'

Tiger

If Faxon is America's best putter on a day in, day out basis, Tiger Woods is undoubtedly one of the finest pressure putters the world has ever known. He, like Jack Nicklaus before him, rates as one of those rare golfers who, when he *has* to hole a putt, does so.

Woods, of course, is a golfaholic when it comes to improving his long and short games but what does he do when his putting is a little off? Believe it or not, just like every other golfer in the game, he messes around on the practice putting green until things improve. 'When things go wrong and the ball is not going in,' he says, 'I kinda fool around with a checklist and eventually you start feeling something that makes the ball come off the putter solidly every time.'

That checklist includes things like balance, posture, alignment, grip pressure, hands too high or too low – all important things for expert players.

Despite his supreme expertise Woods, like Alliss and Faxon, recognizes the value of keeping things simple and the top Tiger putting tip is straightforward. 'The eyes must be parallel to the target line,' he says. 'I find that if I cock my head to the left or the right at address even slightly I'll subconsciously steer the putter head in the direction my eyes are aligned. So I like to use the bill of my baseball cap as a reference point. If it's parallel to the target line, I know my eyes are parallel also – providing I put my cap on straight!'

Too many putts?

Some of the world's top players have reputations as great putters while some of them regard their performance on the greens as their weak point. Through all his successful years Nicklaus was seen as a man who, if he had an important putt of 15 feet and under, would always hole it. That ability to sink putts when he had to was a large part of the reason why he won 18 major professional championships, more than anyone else in history. Nowadays Woods is generally regarded in the same vein – when he putts well, he wins. Seve Ballesteros, even when he lost his long game, was still a genius on (and around) the greens and in common with other great putters, all three were blessed with (or developed) a seemingly uncanny ability to will the ball into the hole.

The mind is a powerful tool in golf but the truth was rather more prosaic than that. They were not afraid of the putt, they were willing to hit it hard enough to have a good chance of going in and they possessed excellent judgement of line, length and strength.

Some really good players have been dogged by an inability to putt consistently throughout their careers. One of the outstanding examples was Mark James, the European Ryder Cup captain of 1999. He was good enough to win 18 times on the European Tour but, although he finished in the top five in the Open Championship four times, he might easily have won a major or two if his putting had been up to the standard of the rest of his game. He must be holing a few nowadays because he has been very successful on the US Champions Tour, the circuit for the over-fifties.

Darren Clarke is another golfer capable of sublime hitting and few, if any, golfers have struck the ball so well up to the moment that they are required to putt. But the Ulsterman is what his fellow professionals call a 'streak' putter: when he's good he's very, very good and when he's bad, well, forget it. At the time of writing Clarke had had two rounds of 60, two of 62 and four of 63 on the European Tour and you cannot score as brilliantly as that without converting your chances by putting superbly. But up to the end of the 2005 season, in a 15-year career, he had won only ten times on the European Tour, nothing like as frequently as his overall game suggests he should have. The sight of Clarke standing and staring at a ball that is sitting on the rim of the hole instead of falling in has, unfortunately for him, been a regular one in Europe, America and around the world.

Putters

Putting fads come and putting fads go and when you've been playing golf for a while, you'll probably find that you've started to accumulate putters of all shapes and sizes as you – and the manufacturers – continue to search for a foolproof way of getting the ball into the hole. Some people never change but others are inveterate tinkerers and become immersed in the never-ending search for the perfect putter. Karsten Solheim, for example, a mechanical design engineer, took up golf, decided he needed to hole more putts and fiddled and fretted away in his garage until he came up with the first Ping putter, so called because of the sound it made when it hit the ball. It worked well but looked ugly and Solheim spent several years haunting the practice putting green at tournaments trying to persuade professionals to use his putters. The invariable reaction was, 'Oh dear, here comes that old man with the goofy putters' but in the mid-1960s, Solheim came up with an implement he called the Ping Anser ('this is the answer') and Julius Boros, twice US Open champion, won the 1967 Phoenix Open with it. 'It looks like a bunch of nuts and bolts welded together,' Boros said, 'but the ball goes in the hole.'

Equipment companies pour millions into research and development nowadays – and there is a bewildering array of putters to choose from, with heads of all shapes and sizes. How do you decide which is the right one for you? Trial and error is the short answer. Try a few out. Don't worry though if your choice is limited or if you have no choice at all. You can still get the ball into the hole. Remember that in the Ryder Cup of 1985, Ben Crenshaw, one of the best putters in the world, broke his putter early on in the singles, then used his sand iron for a couple of holes before putting with his 1-iron for the rest of the match. He only lost to Eamonn Darcy on the last green.

Choosing a putter

Pick a putter that you like the look of – if you don't like looking at the head when it's behind the ball, you'll not be in the right frame of mind to use it well.

How does it sit behind the ball? Check that the sole is flat on the ground and that the head doesn't want to twist to one side. You'll want it to sit comfortably so that you can take it back and through with a minimum of fuss.

Is it the right length for you? Can you stand comfortably, arms hanging loosely from the shoulders, not too crouched or cramped (unless that's the style you've chosen)? Does the grip feel comfortable – not too thick, not too thin?

Have a few swishes, hit a few putts and remember that there are as many putting styles as there are players putting. Everyone's different but never forget the object of the exercise: to get the ball into the hole. The fewer putts you have the better your score.

Two-ball drill: Place two balls about 18 inches (45 cm) apart and hit one into the other so that the second ball rolls in a straight line without shooting off at a tangent. It's a good way to develop a feel for striking the ball squarely and consistently.

Yips

A chapter on putting wouldn't be complete without a brief talk about the yips or what the great Tom Watson, winner of the Open five times, called the flinches. They are one and the same thing and should be spared any golfer and not wished on your worst enemy. They are included here simply because they exist and you're bound to encounter people who suffer from what can only be described as an abhorrent affliction.

The yips are not simply a failure of nerve: they are a phobia and are generally regarded as incurable (although neurolinguistic programming holds out some hope of improvement). Henry Longhurst, the great television commentator and essayist, who lived in the days before NLP, summed up the problem: 'Once you've had 'em, you've got 'em.'

Put simply, a yip is an inability to get the ball into the hole even from distances as short as 18 inches. It is a freezing first of the mental and then of the physical faculties, with the golfer standing over a short putt and being totally unable to bring himself to take the putter back. Eventually, the mind tells the rest of the body that this is ridiculous and that the putter must be moved in order to make the ball move and what follows next is often nightmarish. The golfer makes a swift, uncontrolled jab at the ball which will then go scurrying off, often 20 feet or more beyond the hole. Or it may only go three feet beyond the hole, at which point the whole problem recurs.

One of the best known sufferers is Bernhard Langer, twice winner of the US Masters and captain of Europe's Ryder Cup team in 2004. At the 17th at Royal Lytham and St Annes in the 1988 Open championship, Langer hit a superb second shot to within three feet of the pin. Then the yips took over and he finished up batting the ball around the hole five times – trying his hardest on every putt – before, almost by accident, it went in.

Langer is an exceptional competitor and by employing extraordinary mental application and adopting a variety of putting techniques (the long putter and the Langer lock, a grip devised to act like a vice, have both been used), he has managed to overcome several bouts of the yips but he is a huge exception to the Longhurst Dictum. It is a far better thing never to experience what is easily the worst affliction that can be encountered in golf.

A word of advice

Yipping is gruesome to watch and the torment of the yipper is well-nigh unimaginable and not to be underestimated by those who are not thus plagued. It's advisable not to watch if you can help it and the golden rule is to keep quiet and say nothing unless asked. It is a very private torment. Missing short putts is not the same as yipping. If you get 'em, you'll know it.

A cautionary tale

It doesn't matter how long you play or how good you become, you're always likely to be tempted to look for 'the secret', that magic something that will unlock the mysteries of the game and its constituent parts. Frank Stranahan, a wealthy American amateur, who was good enough to finish second alongside Byron Nelson behind Jimmy Demaret in the 1947 Masters and won the Amateur championship (British version) in 1948 and 1950, was never content. In Dermot Gilleece's book *Breaking 80: The life and times of Joe Carr*, Carr, the great Irish amateur, recalled an incident prior to the 1951 Walker Cup at Royal Birkdale. He and Willie Turnesa, the US captain, were sitting in the clubhouse when Stranahan, who was having trouble with his putting came in in some despair and the following exchange took place:

'Gee Willie, I can't seem to get the ball into the hole.'
'Well you know Frank, putting is all about movement.'
'Well yes but...'
'By the way Frank, do you breathe while you putt?'
'Sure I do.'
'That could be the problem.'

Carr continued: 'So, off Frank went, sure he had found the answer, only to return in about half an hour, his face red as a beetroot from holding his breath. "It doesn't seem to make any difference, Willie," he moaned, despairingly. Then Willie, the personification of patience, suggested: "What you have to do Frank, is make the stroke between heartbeats."

'It took some time but Frank eventually realized he was being had. And in common with the rest of us, he accepted that there was no magic cure for putting problems.'

Carr, who won numerous championships, including the Amateur three times, and played in ten Walker Cup matches, was not always the most reliable of putters and Sir Michael Bonallack, himself one of the world's great amateurs (and a phenomenal putter) remembered the 1959 Walker Cup at Muirfield: 'Joe was putting with a rusty headed, hickory shafted implement which looked as if it had been found in a rubbish tip. Having missed one or two short putts with it while playing in the foursomes with Guy Wolstenholme, he was walking off the green when an over-eager young spectator, running to get a good view, trod on the putter shaft and broke it. Joe was upset, especially as his partner remarked: "Thank heavens for that." Thereafter he putted with a 3-iron with much better results.'

The end of the world

A good short game makes you a match for anyone and it can be incredibly irritating and nerve-wracking if an opponent is forever leaving long putts or chips dead (so close to the hole that they can't miss the next one) or even holing them. Good putters and chippers aren't just *hoping* to hole out, they're *expecting* to and they do so often enough for you to realize that it's not a fluke: it's skill.

To be that good, you have to get the ball up to the hole but as Dr Karl Morris, one of Europe's leading sports psychologists and a consultant to the PGA, says: 'Far too many golfers leave putts and short chips woefully short and the ball never has a chance to go in the hole. Why is that?

The problem is about focus: golfers tend to see the front lip of the hole as being the end of the known universe; they never see beyond the hole. Imagine if we still thought that the earth was flat and Edinburgh was at the edge, most of us wouldn't ever get to Edinburgh let alone ever see the Highlands.

To highlight what I mean try this experiment: stand on the putting green a reasonable distance from the hole, about ten paces or so, look at the hole, then turn your putter upside down, close your eyes and walk to the hole. The game is to place the putter on the ground where you think the hole is – without looking. No peeking.

I have tried this with hundreds of golfers and more than 95 per cent of them come up way short. Amazingly, the good putters tend to get past the hole.

Next time you putt look at the hole and then see *beyond* it. Actually look *past* the hole. This change of perspective will allow you to stroke the ball with enough pace to get past the hole as opposed to tentatively dribbling the ball to the edge. Dave Pelz, the short game guru, has stated that an ideal putt would travel 17 inches (43 cm) past the hole if it missed. This new vision of life beyond the hole will allow that.'

05

setting to

Tip at the top

Let the club do the work.

The one thing that is obvious and indisputable about golf is that in order to play it we have to have clubs. There was a time when Sir Winston Churchill was able, with a fair degree of accuracy, to describe the game rather dismissively thus: 'Trying to knock a tiny ball into an even smaller hole with implements ill-suited to their purpose.'

However, that was decades ago and now the implements available are very much suited to their purpose, although it may take a while before the beginner totally accepts this. Just remember that whatever its intricacies – and it can be made to sound very complicated indeed – golf is essentially a simple game. For Henry Cotton, three times Open champion and a teacher of note, after more than 50 years in the game, good, consistent golf boiled down to 'the ability to find the back of the ball with the clubhead square'. Too much golfing shorthand? We hope this book will help you understand the concept and that your own experiments and experience will give you a feel for it. Your aim is to bring the club into contact with the ball in such a way that it results in a cleanly hit shot. A club is not an alien implement of torture, it is a useful and necessary tool that you can learn to use well if you want to.

Start right

Luther Blacklock, an Advanced Fellow of the PGA who has been the professional at Woburn for many years, is adamant that the correct equipment is vital. 'Imagine a six-foot adult trying to learn to ride on a bike designed for a six-year-old. It would make the learning process extremely difficult and could lead to injury. It cannot be overstated how important it is to learn golf with clubs that are the correct length and weight for each individual. Do not fall into the trap of thinking, "I'm just a beginner so it doesn't matter what clubs I have as long as they're inexpensive". The correct equipment will encourage the correct swing for your physique, accelerating the learning curve whilst minimizing the risk of injury. You do not need a big outlay and it is possible to get further good advice at no initial cost. Go to any PGA professional (you don't need to be a member of the club) and he or she can talk you through the early decisions and set you on a safe and steady path. He or she can assess your needs and in most cases can lend you trial clubs to suit your age, physique and gender.

Whatever money you spend eventually can be on an informed basis. It would be far better to spend £100 on second-hand clubs that fit you as opposed to £500 on shiny new clubs that do not. Most professionals will lend a novice pupil a club at the outset of a course of lessons, so remember: consult and try before you buy.'

Start small

To begin with you do not need a full set. A full set comprises 14 clubs, usually four woods, nine irons and a putter. The woods used to be made of wood and the name has stuck but these days they will almost certainly be made of metal and many people, particularly those of us who do not have the strength or skill to use long irons effectively, will have more than four. But at first, in order to get the feel of hitting a ball, you need only one club, a 7-iron for example and preferably a putter.

To tackle a course you'll want a few more clubs but you need no more than a 3- or 5-wood, 5-, 7- and 9-irons, perhaps a wedge, and a putter – just six of the 14 allowed. Annika Sorenstam, the Swede who is in the process of proving herself the best woman golfer the world has ever known, started with just a half set, sharing with her sister Charlotta. Annika took the odd-numbered clubs, Charlotta the evens. As a child Seve Ballesteros practised endlessly on the beach at Pedrena with a battered old 3-iron, the only club he had. By the time he acquired a full set the dashing Spaniard could do anything he wanted to do with a golf ball and went on to have one of the game's great careers.

Loft

The fact is that the clubs all have different degrees of loft, with not a lot between them and it will not be until real proficiency is achieved that a player can take full advantage of a complete set.

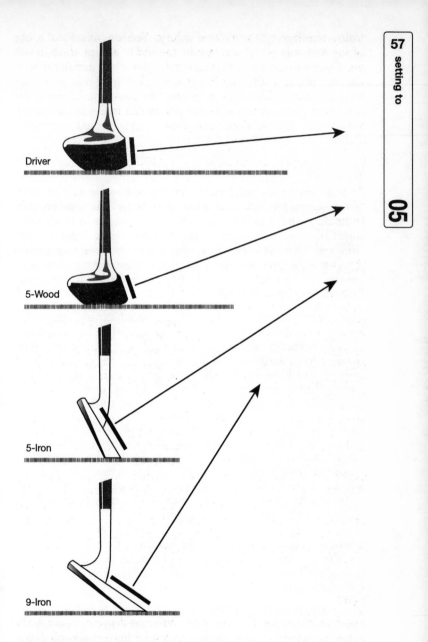

figure 5.1 different clubs will have a different trajectory

Loft is the degree of angle at which the clubhead is set and is one of the determining factors in how far and how high the ball will go. The more loft the higher the flight of the ball and the shorter the distance it will travel. For instance, a 5-iron will go further than a 9-iron, which will go higher. As you progress, you will learn how far you hit each club and which one you use where. (There are few hard-and-fast rules and personal preference counts for a lot.) Even when you have all 14 clubs, there will be many days when you do not use all of them. In fact, since having back trouble Patricia rarely carries more than ten.

So start small. You can build a full set when your golf becomes more accomplished and you can enjoy all the modern technology that has made present-day golf clubs so much more forgiving than they were in the bad old days. Gone are the 'stingers' – a nerve-numbing feeling – that you used to get when a ball was hit hard into the ground and gone, for the most part, are the woeful results that stem from hitting the ball well away from the centre of the club.

This improvement is thanks to a manufacturing technique known as perimeter weighting – a process that means what it says. By spreading the weight of the clubhead around the edges, the area from which a good shot is possible – the so-called sweet spot – is much enlarged. This in turn means that what in the old days would have been a weak and feeble effort now not only goes further but often actually looks like a half-decent shot.

In our household this is known as a 'tick' or 'T-Y-K', which stands for 'Thank You Karsten' after Karsten Solheim, the inventor of Ping golf clubs and the man who popularized perimeter weighting. The technique has spread through the game and, as it has done so, clubs have gone from the old, standard clubhead size, which now looks tiny, to midsize to oversize, with better shots being progressively more and more available as the size of the clubhead grows. All the manufacturers now use perimeter weighting for what are known as 'game improvement' clubs and rather like the fact that nowadays there are not really any bad cars, there are no bad golf clubs either.

There are, though, clubs that are more suitable for one person than another and this is a matter for experimentation on the practice ground or the driving range and for consultation with a professional. Not long ago Dai (David), having already lost the match, borrowed the driver (a Wilson Staff) one of his opponents had been using and promptly hit the ball 20 yards

(18 m) past his previous best effort that day. Golf being golf, that club became a must-have, although the search for the magic weapon never really stops – and a trial of more than one shot is advisable before buying.

Suit yourself

It used to be the case that newcomers to the game used hand-me-downs, clubs inherited from father or granny or friend of friend and often, in the case of women, from husband. The snag was that it was mostly a matter of sheer chance as to whether the inheritor got clubs suitable for their shape or size or swing speed and the women especially always got a raw deal. The number of times their husband's clubs would be suitable might be one in a thousand. Nine hundred and ninety nine times the women would be lumbered with something too heavy and with the wrong type of shaft and be condemned to hitting poor shots through no fault of their own.

Nowadays the women's market is a sector that no manufacturer can dare to ignore and there is a choice almost as wide as that for men. The same principles apply, in that the size and shape of the person using the club does matter as, of course, does their ability. But the woman beginner should take care not to start with some cast-offs found in the garage. If they are men's clubs and too heavy, with too stiff a shaft, she could acquire some bad habits before hitting a shot in anger. Clubs should help not hinder.

Your needs will almost certainly change as you improve and become stronger and more adept – and in the case of children start getting taller. Patricia built up a set of much-loved Jessie Valentines (no longer made but named after the diminutive Scottish golfer who became one of the first women professionals), getting a club for her birthday, another for Christmas, perhaps even saving her pocket money. She loved those clubs but one day she started topping and couldn't stop. Even her favourite 7-iron was no longer infallible. Eventually, the realization dawned: the clubs were too short; she'd grown too tall for them and needed longer clubs.

Toots

Henry Cotton, for all his nous and expertise, fell foul of his wife's improving swing and ability. He was married to a diminutive, feisty Argentine called Toots and in *Thanks For The Game* recalled an uncomfortable moment: 'Her first clubs were short "ladies-weight" ones, as I was taught suited most women, and she did reasonably well with them. Then one day she was watching me practise and picked up one of my clubs and hit a ball with it. It went 20 yards (18 m) further. "Oh!" was the reaction. "So you didn't want me to improve, I can see." Was I embarrassed? It took me years to live this down.'

The ultimate secret?

Cotton had an interesting theory on teaching women and wrote: 'Eventually I got her [Toots] to play quite decently, mainly by telling her she was no good, had no chance, and so on. (I think this is the only way to tell any woman to do something you want her to do – tell her she can't. It still works 50 years later!)'

Clubs for kids

There are large numbers of children coming into the game these days and it's good to start early because kids have no preconceived notions about what they can and can not do. There are plastic clubs for toddlers and Tri-Golf, a game developed by the Golf Foundation to encourage tots to have a hit, uses plastic clubs with big heads and large foam balls that don't hurt, so the players can run around willy-nilly having fun. It won't be long, though, before they want to use the real thing and there are now plenty of clubs made specifically for young girls and boys. In the old days they would make do with an adult set cut down but that was rarely satisfactory, with the cutting down destroying the balance of the club, thus making the hitting of a good shot more accidental than intentional. It makes sense to provide children with proper equipment and this is an important segment of the market because if they're hooked on the game young, they'll continue playing for life. It's also where the Sergio Garcias of the future come from.

The Spaniard, now such a thrilling star in world golf, was small for his age but he started swinging a golf club almost as soon as he could walk. Being the son of a professional, his father Victor helped, of course, but no chances were taken. At every stage of his physical development, Sergio was given the right clubs for his size and by the time he was 15 years old he was playing senior golf for his country. Peter McEvoy, a Walker Cup player and captain, remembers playing for England against him and says: 'He was still quite small and it almost seemed as though he should be in short trousers but he was technically very good and could hit the ball as far as anyone else.' This only happened because he had been nurtured at every age and given expert advice, and also because he himself loved playing and competing. As Lynn Marriott and Pia Nilsson, two of the best, most thoughtful coaches around, say in their helpful and wise booklet *Golf parent for the future*: 'They [the children] are human beings who play golf, not just golfers who happen to be human beings!'

Built just for you

Once you've decided that you want to keep playing and can hit the ball reasonably well and have enough money to buy some clubs of your own, the best route is to consult a custom-fitting centre. A lot of professionals provide this service and it's worth making the effort to seek one out. The technology now is amazing and there are machines that will accurately measure the type of swing you have and determine from that and other data just which clubs would be perfect for you. There's a lot to consider – length, weight, grip, loft, lie, type of shaft – so expert help makes sense.

In the early days of golf, when shafts were made of hickory (a member of the walnut family), the variances between clubs that were supposed to be exactly the same were often enormous. All a player could go on was 'feel' – how the club felt in his hands before and during a shot. It often took years to identify a full set and if one of the clubs broke, it could take years to find a replacement. At one time, before restrictions came into being, Bobby Jones, the legendary amateur from the 1920s and 1930s, had 30 hickory-shafted clubs in his bag which, if nothing else, made life hell for his caddie. But because of the limited effectiveness of the clubs of that day, Jones perceived a need for all of them.

The 14-club restriction came about because things were getting out of hand and now there are strict penalties for carrying more than the allotted number. Ian Woosnam, the 2006 Ryder Cup captain and former Masters champion, was one of the most notable victims. Playing in the Open Championship at Royal Lytham and St Annes in 2001, the Welshman opened with a birdie at the first hole of the final round to put himself in strong contention for the title. Then, on the 2nd tee, his caddie said words which have never been truer: 'You're going to go ballistic.' Miles Byrne, the caddie, informed Woosie that they had two drivers in the bag, making 15 clubs in all and that meant a two-stroke penalty.

Byrne was right. Woosnam, seeing his chance of winning the Open receding before his eyes, did go ballistic. A cleaned-up version of what he said would be, 'it's the only thing I ask you to do,' meaning count the clubs on the first tee precisely to avoid the situation that had just arisen. Woosnam, who had been practising with two drivers, hurled one of them into the undergrowth, hurled invective at all and sundry and went on to finish joint third. It was one of golf's great 'if onlys'. Without the two-stroke penalty he would have been second and won £218,333 more than he actually took away: an expensive mistake. Shortly afterwards Byrne retired from caddying.

In the bag

Jones would not have been popular with the game's first caddies, back in the 1800s, when a player's clubs were carried loose under the arm. Eventually fairly primitive stovepipe bags evolved and from them we have the enormous cabin trunk-style bags favoured by today's tournament professionals, who need to have every conceivable piece of equipment with them at all times. They also have a caddie to lug them around and if you think those guys are not fit, just try lifting a fully kitted out tournament bag, never mind carting it around for 18 holes. They are simply not necessary for anybody else.

All the average amateur requires is a lightweight bag fitted with a two-pronged support that enables it to rest on two legs instead of having to be laid on the ground. These bags are extremely tough, very light and, with the recent innovation of double shoulder straps, very easy to carry. Using a bag with just one strap has an unbalancing effect, which is more tiring and means an added strain on whichever side of the body gets the bulk of the work. This can put extra stress on the lower back – and back problems are something that no golfer wants.

Be sensible, learn to understand your own body's limitations and aches and pains and how to prevent or counteract them. Don't forget the value of contra exercise – that is working in the opposite direction. For example, if you are right-handed and practising a lot, take time to swing left-handed occasionally and vice versa. You don't have to hit balls, just give the body a change and a rest. As in most things balance is the key.

Carrying your clubs is not a chore as long as you don't overload yourself. Your bag should be light and have enough pockets for most contingencies. You will need one pocket for golf balls, a smaller one for tees, markers, pencils and divot repairers and a largish one into which you should be able to squeeze a lightweight waterproof jacket and hat or cap in case of sudden showers. (If you're playing in the northern winter, you'll probably have all your waterproofs and woollies on before you go out.) There should also be a little pouch to hold a bottle of water. Get the balance right and a lightweight bag will enable you to walk the golf course in some comfort which, after all, is part of the exercise.

If you are physically unable to carry your own clubs or are of an age where you get too tired you can always use a trolley. These are carts for your bag and those who are getting on in years or cannot travel light find them useful, especially the powered versions that operate from a battery and do not require any pulling. But you will find that carrying your clubs makes for a quicker and easier round of golf – you can walk over a green for instance but must take a trolley around it – and a pull trolley is certainly not the answer if the course is hilly. A bag slung across your back is much easier.

On your feet

Shoes are terribly important and you must get these right or you will not have any comfort at all. An 18-hole golf course is about a five-mile walk and is no place to be if every step is agony. The modern golf shoe is far superior to its predecessor, which tended to start out heavy and, when wet, became tiringly so. Nowadays there is a myriad of choice and most shoes are light, showerproof at the very least and are fitted with soft spikes. These are rubber clusters of small spikes that have replaced the simple, single metal spike and are now compulsory at a great many golf courses. The reason is that soft spikes do not dig up the surface of the greens in the way that metal ones do, which in turn means that putting is both easier and fairer.

Perhaps the best illustration of the problems that spike marks can cause is what happened to Bernhard Langer when he was playing for Europe in the Ryder Cup against the Americans at Kiawah Island, in South Carolina, in 1991. His was the last match and it came down to one simple act: could he hole a five-foot (one and a half metres) putt which would win the Cup for Europe? Normally the betting would be that this experienced campaigner, with nerves of steel, would manage to somehow get this incredibly pressure-laden putt into the hole. But as he inspected the putt, he spotted a spike mark sticking up on his exact line to the hole, a mark that might be big enough to divert the ball from its intended path. The rules didn't allow him to tap the mark down, so Langer had to try and avoid the spike mark and still find a way into the hole – and he failed. The ball just missed, Europe had lost the Ryder Cup by a single point and Langer threw back his head and howled his disappointment and distress.

Balls

There was a time when a golf ball was a precious thing. For many years after the Second World War they were hardly a priority as Britain struggled to return to normality and they were so scarce that the thought of losing one was abhorrent. Many a time you would see a fourball searching an area in line abreast, first up and down and then across, leaving, literally, no blade of grass unturned. To lose a ball in those days might mean having to give in and go back to the clubhouse.

Thankfully things are very different now, with balls in plentiful supply in most places and the incentive these days for finding your ball is not to incur the penalty stroke that comes with losing it. It pays to keep a close eye on its progress – however annoyed you are with your errant shot – and mark where it lands as carefully as you can.

Top-level players very rarely lose a ball but it does occasionally happen and did, famously, to Tiger Woods in the Open championship at Royal St George's in 2003. He hit his opening drive of the first round into an area of long, thick, tangled rough and although a small army of marshals looked for the prescribed five minutes for it, the ball remained hidden. Woods had to go back to the tee and play another which, oddly enough, went to almost the same area as the first but which this time was spotted by that army of marshals. The American said afterwards that it was the first time he had lost a ball in seven years of professional golf. As, in that period, he would have played approximately 640 rounds of competitive golf, that is some record.

Woods is one of a small number of top-level professionals who have their golf balls made specially for them by the manufacturer to whom they are affiliated. The vast majority of tournament professionals – and the top amateurs – all play with their preferred ball, which will be any one of the many different types that can be bought in a professional's shop.

There are balls made specifically to go further, balls which accept spin more readily and balls which are a compromise between the two. There are balls that are constructed as two-piece balls, three-piece, even four-piece; there are wound balls, perimeter-weighted balls, surlyn, balata, metal mix and even titanium balls – none of which it is necessary to know about at first.

There is also, naturally enough, a range of different prices, but for the beginner the most expensive balls are an unnecessary luxury. The top-of-the-range balls possess characteristics that only the top-of-the-range golfers can benefit from, so pay what your pocket feels most comfortable with. As you get more experienced, you can experiment with different varieties and decide which ball you prefer.

The collector

There is a species of person, more common in America than anywhere else, that regards golf not so much as a sport but as an opportunity to 'collect' golf courses. For these people money is rarely any object and they are prepared to spend vast sums travelling the world playing, and therefore collecting, famous courses. And it's the collecting that counts not the playing.

One year we were at Kiawah Island, waiting to play the Ocean course, which had hosted the famous – or more accurately infamous – Ryder Cup match of 1991. On the 1st tee we were joined by a collector, who had travelled all the way from Oklahoma to South Carolina to add another golfing notch to his belt. Just why he bothered is a mystery. He was a terrible golfer, yet insisted on playing from the furthermost back tees, so giving himself shots he was just not capable of playing. There were times when he could not hit the ball far enough to reach the fairway and that, at Kiawah, means you are in a marsh and have lost your ball to the alligators.

As a result of this idiocy he not only lost 27 golf balls that day – all of them brand new and top quality – but we also took six hours to play 18 holes, held up the entire course and by about the 8th had stopped speaking altogether. Just what that Oklahoman got out of it is totally unfathomable – although he undoubtedly set a personal best in balls lost.

That's one of the dangers of collecting – it can become an obsession and people do daft things. Like the guy who flew thousands of miles to Ireland, drove to Royal Portrush, one of the world's great courses, on the north Antrim coast, paid a green fee, walked onto the course and kept walking until he reached the 14th, a famous par three called Calamity, played it twice, walked back in and left. It was on his list of great holes to play and he wasn't going to be diverted from his quest by the rest of the course. At least he wasn't inconveniencing anybody else.

Golf lends itself to collecting – clubs, cards, balls, ball markers, memorabilia of all sorts, courses by a particular architect (Colt, Mackenzie, Fowler, Trent Jones for example) – but don't forget the game. Travelling to play new courses is part of the fun and to do so in the company of friends is one of the greatest pleasures that the game offers. A week or more playing courses that offer a different challenge can be absolutely wonderful but be sure to go because you want to play golf in good company on a good course and not solely to tick a place off your list.

Know your limits

Whatever your reasons for going and whatever else you do, be sure to play from tees that your game can manage. The professionals play from the back tees because they can drive the ball 280 yards (256 m) or more, straight, every time. Very few people can do that, which is why there are tees in more friendly and accessible areas. They are not for wimps, they are for the vast majority of golfers, so we should use them.

Practising with a purpose

If you become in any way serious about the game you will want to practise the tips and drills that the top coaches present in this book. If you are a member of a club with a practice ground, you are in luck but if not there will probably be a driving range somewhere within a reasonable distance. The trick is not to go there and just whale away at the ball, hoping to get it airborne and in vaguely the right direction. Practice has to be done with a purpose and there is plenty of advice on how to do that in these pages.

But do practise. It is the key to improvement. Half an hour or so spent hitting balls or playing a few holes, concentrating on a particular aspect of your game, with a target in mind, will be far more valuable to you (if you want to improve) than endless rounds of hacking around doing the same old thing. Gary Player, who won nine major championships, overcoming the physical handicap of being both small and slightly built and the technical handicap of starting out with a dreadful grip and a faulty swing, used to say: 'You know, the more I practise, the luckier I get.'

In that one sentence he put down those observers who initially thought he was fortunate to win some tournaments, and he also emphasized to the world how important a solid and regular practice routine is.

It was Jack Nicklaus, back in the 1960s, who also pointed out the value of practice. To the astonishment, in those days, of the other competitors, Nicklaus would go round in a 66, or similar, and then go the practice ground. When asked what he could possibly have to work on after such a good round Nicklaus would reply that he wanted to cement the good things he had been doing, not eliminate the bad. It was a new concept in golf but it took root immediately and now every tournament professional automatically goes to the range after a round, for one reason or another.

The hardest worker in world golf, certainly among the top professionals, has long been Vijay Singh. The Fijian, who got to the top of the world rankings in 2004–5, has been known to spend all day on the practice range – and be late home for dinner. Woods, far from resting on his dominance, frequently will spend all morning hitting balls and all afternoon playing 18 holes, while Britain's Nick Faldo would admit to having been obsessed by the challenge of trying to attain perfection. He, like Woods and anyone who has ever played the game, knows that such a thing is not possible, but the fun lies in the attempt.

For the average player practice is not only beneficial, it can be deeply satisfying. For instance, as your game progresses you will find that on the practice ground or at the range it is possible to hit a series of, say, 20 or 30 7-iron shots that are as good as you can do. You simply do not get the chance to do that on the golf course, where each shot demands a different club. The danger, though, is that you will start to just whack balls aimlessly into the air and even the best are not immune.

Dave Musgrove, one of Britain's super-caddies, who has worked with Seve Ballesteros, Sandy Lyle and Lee Janzen, was once watching Janzen hit balls on the range and realized that his boss was not really concentrating. Muzzy pointed out that while the last shot had looked quite good, it would probably have finished deep in the trees if his boss had hit it on the first hole in the tournament. Janzen quickly realized that he was not aiming at anything – it was literally aimless practice – and changed his ways. He started picking out a target for every shot and went on to win the tournament and almost a million dollars – and Musgrove was able to pay off his mortgage.

Nowadays the likes of the rising English star Luke Donald tend to practise with every club in the bag first and then 'play' the first three, and last three, of the holes on that day's course. In other words, if the first hole requires a drive and 5-iron, Donald will hit those clubs on the practice ground and if the second needs a 3-wood off the tee, followed by a 9-iron, he will hit those – and so on. 'By the time I get to the first tee,' says Donald, 'I've got no worries because I've already played the hole in practice.'

You can do that too. Just because we don't hit the ball like a pro doesn't mean that we can't think like one.

Canny practising

Ian D. Rae, the SGU (Scottish Golf Union) national coach, has this handy tip for those of us who don't have too much time to practise – or lack single-minded dedication and get bored easily. This method also has the advantage of ensuring that your three main sessions are extremely fruitful. Ian suggests: 'If you have an hour to practise on the range or the practice area, it's best to make the time as productive as possible. If you lash the driver from the first ball to the last, it will only be a physical workout with no benefit to your game. Try splitting your time so you only have to concentrate in short spells on one thing. This will give your game more chance to improve and will be more fun and the break between the 12-minute sessions should improve the work you do in those sessions. To begin with you can hit most of your shots from a tee peg, then put the ball on the grass (or mat) and keep switching between the two to build confidence. Here's a timetable for an hour's practice.

- 7 minutes warming up, starting with a wedge
- 12 minutes on the shot or skill you are trying to work on (weight distribution, for example) (A)
- 5 minutes doing something totally different (pitching, chipping, putting, having a cup of coffee) (B)
- 12 minutes on A (weight distribution)
- 5 minutes on B (something different)
- 12 minutes on A (weight distribution)
- 7 minutes warming down, hitting short clubs to finish
  Total: 60 minutes

You can change the timings depending on how much time you have to practise but stick with the same principle and you'll keep yourself interested and your practice effective.'

06
heading for the course

In this chapter you will learn:
- what to wear
- how to navigate a course
- the dos and don'ts.

Tip at the top

No need to get hot under the collar.

Life being what it is you'll undoubtedly end up heading for a golf course sooner rather than later irrespective of the state of your game – and it doesn't matter how long you've been playing, the state of your game will not always be immaculate. Sometimes it will be downright dire and drive you to despair but there'll always be a vestige of hope to cling on to – a perfect pitch, an exquisite escape or a cracker of a drive. You won't always be in control of your game and that's fine, everyone who plays golf understands that. What you can be in control of is how you behave on the course, how you get yourself round, so that you and everyone else can enjoy it as much as possible.

Clothes

First of all, a brief word on what to wear. To play well you need to be comfortable, with the freedom to swing and move freely. Thanks to materials like lycra and elastane that doesn't have to mean loose-fitting gear and you can be as stylish as you wish, while bearing in mind some dress codes are stricter than others.

Many clubs love to plaster the place with edicts on what and what not to wear, some of them laughable. Golf clubs are particularly devoted to shirts with collars for some baffling reason but if you stick with smart casual, you should be alright. We could write a whole book on dress codes and attitudes to attire but if you want to be on the safe side, just call the club you're going to and ask. And don't worry about it too much. The game's the thing.

How to behave

At some point early in a would-be golfer's introduction to the game, someone is bound to utter the word etiquette. It is one of those high-falutin' words for what, in golf, is actually an essential concept. The dictionary definition of etiquette is that it stands for 'the conventional rules of social behaviour', which it sums up as 'politeness' and 'good manners' and in those last two definitions we have all we need to play golf in an acceptable manner.

There are a few dos and don'ts but essentially if you are reasonably polite to those on the course with you and exercise a reasonable degree of good manners, you'll be fine. That doesn't mean that within your own game there cannot be the usual amount of joshing or general winding up that goes on in all friendly sport, simply that there are generally accepted boundaries that are different from football or other games where you can leap about trying to put other people off and spectators boo and hiss and shout abuse. Try something similar on a golf course and you'll be off it pretty quick.

In golf you must always give your opponent (however much you loathe him and want to beat him) the best chance possible of playing his shot. That means remaining silent and out of vision – or out of his line of sight – while he is concentrating on his shot. Golf is a demanding game and it requires, not unreasonably, that fellow players allow that concentration to be uninterrupted. Of course some people's concentration is more fragile than others' and experience will teach you what you can do with whom and when. A complete no-no is what Jose Maria Olazabal did when he was playing a match in his first British boys' championship. He stood inches from his opponent, who was settling to play his shot, and glared at him fiercely. The startled lad complained, Olazabal was told that he had taken competitiveness too far and was imposing himself on a match too literally and must allow his opponents some space. The Spaniard is now generally regarded as a model competitor: fierce but fair.

Silence and stillness are such an important part of the game that there have been matches, often for big money, where one player backs himself to beat a much better player, not with the aid of handicap strokes but with the help of half a dozen coughs. What is more, the better player always loses and the poorer player never uses all his coughs. One way that it works is that when the better player goes to drive off the first tee, his opponent will wait until he gets to the top of his backswing and then cough very loudly. This may or may not put him off his stroke – he may have been expecting it – but what is certain is that he will be expecting it on every stroke thereafter. The trick is not to cough again for several holes while the poor man worries himself into a frenzy wondering when the cough will come again. He is usually five down after six holes and a mental wreck.

This serves to emphasize the need to play the game in the spirit that the rule book actually suggests. The first paragraph of *The Rules of Golf* says: 'The overriding principle is that consideration should be shown to others at all times.' The second paragraph expands on that, saying: 'Unlike many sports, golf is played, for the most part, without the supervision of a referee or umpire. The game relies on *the integrity of the individual* [our italics] to show consideration for other players and to abide by the rules.'

There is more. The Royal and Ancient Golf Club of St Andrews (or to be strictly correct R&A Rules Limited), who make the rules for most of the world, bar the United States and Mexico, says: 'All players should conduct themselves in a disciplined manner, demonstrating courtesy and sportsmanship at all times, irrespective of how competitive they may be.'

You may think that some of Tiger Woods's antics in celebrating his many victories would breach the latter suggestion – and many people, often derided as traditionalists or old-fashioned or just old, would agree with that. Swinging big left hooks into the air as a putt falls into the hole seems to have become acceptable at the top professional level – and Woods has the full respect of his peers – but do it at your local club and you may quickly find yourself on the wrong end of a more serious left hook from one of your playing partners. One man's ebullience is another man's obnoxiousness, so best leave all that until you become the world No. 1.

Basic course craft

One of the big problems faced by a beginner is having the confidence to take his or her game onto the golf course with better players. The fear of holding them up, of doing something 'wrong' or committing some terrible mistake often holds the learner back, which is a pity because the best way to learn is by playing with someone who knows more than you do. Ideally, you should choose a time when it's not too busy and you can learn the basics in a relaxed fashion without fretting about anything else. Try not to rush. If you feel hustled by the people behind, call them through – step aside and wave them to play on – so that you can proceed at your own pace and absorb the fundamental principles of working your way around a golf course. It may all seem baffling, even daunting at first but it won't take long before it becomes second nature and if you get things right from the beginning, it makes life so much easier. A lot of it is common sense.

The Rules of Golf

The Rules of Golf is a compact little book packed with information, a lot of it indispensable, quite a lot of it incomprehensible – especially at this early stage – but it should be in every player's golf bag (it's free, the R&A having persuaded Rolex to sponsor it). It should also be referred to but you won't be alone if you never open it from one year to the next. The danger of that, of course, is that it leaves you at the mercy of people who think they know the rules but don't, but for the moment we'll confine ourselves to a summation of pages 19–22. They outline what's safe and acceptable whenever and wherever you play golf.

Look before you swing

'Players should ensure that no one is standing close by or in a position to be hit by the club or the ball...when they make a stroke or practice swing.'

This is a golden rule because clubs and balls can hurt – even kill. Whenever you swing the club but particularly if you're swishing near the first tee to loosen up, check around first. Make sure there's no one behind you in danger of being hit by you. Always, always check. Make sure it becomes second nature. And if someone else is whirling away indiscriminately, let them know that there are other people about.

When you're on the tee, the person or people you're playing with should normally be standing to the side where you can see them (if you're a left-hander, they'll usually end up behind you), level with you or just back a bit but *not* in front of you. There are exceptions to this rule when you're out on the course but always keep an eye on the person who's hitting the ball and *keep out of the way*. In general, you should all be safe if you take up this position, no matter how erratic or unskilled the person hitting the ball. Bear in mind though that there is often no telling what will happen next.

Giving it some welly

Once, when four of us were still learning the game, we went to a local municipal which had just re-opened after a week of particularly heavy rain. One of us decided to use footwear appropriate for the occasion (wellington boots) and although we all knew it was hardly proper golfing gear, we sneaked him onto the first tee while the pro wasn't looking. When it was his turn to drive he got a bit caught up in his raincoat and smacked the ball hard straight along the ground. It hit the marker post for the ladies' tee several yards in front of us, ricocheted high into the air, flew sharply backwards towards us and, with almost surgical precision, went straight down his wellies. There was only a second or two of stunned silence before all four of us became hysterical with laughter and even the pro, attracted by the noise, eventually saw the funny side of it. However, he wouldn't let our man play on in his wellies, so he had to go home and get some proper shoes.

Hold your fire

'Players should not play until the players in front are out of range.'

At some courses there'll be a starter on the first tee to tell you when to go but for the rest of the round it'll be up to you to judge. If you think your absolute best, known in the trade as a Number 1 stonker, would scatter the people in front, it's best to wait, even if experience tells you that they're in no danger whatsoever.

Sod's law dictates that if you elect to go too soon, you'll hit the stonker. Sometimes the people in front will have been faffing about to such an extent that you let rip before they've left the green. Don't. It's dangerous and could go horribly wrong. Instead practise the deep breathing that is the sine qua non of equable golf. Breathing is essential for life but it's amazing how often we forget to do it and where better to remember than on a golf course, where there's plenty of fresh air and we're playing a game that lends itself to a calm, measured approach.

Lenny's lift

This only takes a few seconds and most important of all it's wonderfully calming. Perfect for those moments of pure frustration. It's a favourite of Lenny Woodhall, who's been a professional trainer for 45 years and has coached numerous boxing champions, including his son Richie and helped those of us who are less physically distinguished get fit for the life we lead.

Stand up straight, relaxed, feet about 12 inches (30 cm) apart, arms hanging loosely by your side. Breathe in deeply through your nose from your stomach (making sure that your tummy button pushes out as you take in oxygen) and as you're breathing in, raise your arms up gently – swinging them out in front of you, then up, keeping them straight – and rise up onto your toes, maintaining your balance without wobbling.

When you're right up on your toes with your arms above your head, breathe out through your mouth and roll your shoulders back and bring your arms gently back down to your sides as you come down off your toes.

The key is to breathe with your feet. In other words, start breathing when your feet start rising and think of your feet controlling your breathing. That's why Lenny likes to call it 'all through breathing', not just because it goes all the way from toe to top but because breathing is vital in everything we do. It's all (done) through breathing.

Shouting allowed

'If a player plays a ball in a direction where there is a danger of hitting someone, a shouted warning should be given. The traditional word in such situations is "fore".'

Fore is an abbreviation of the word 'before', meaning the players before you. Errant shots are inevitable, balls ricochet off trees, people make misjudgements, so whenever you hear what will become a very familiar yell, duck and cover your head with your hands. Don't stand tall and look around going, 'Where? Where? Does that mean us?' You may end up feeling daft if the cry is directed at another group or person entirely but better that than a big bruise or something considerably worse.

Learn to keep an eye on what's going on around you and notice who might be within range – people playing an adjoining hole, for example or using a public right of way. If you watch golf on the telly or go to a tournament, you'll notice that the pros and caddies don't always shout but use a form of semaphore, shooting out an arm, left or right, depending on direction. In that case it's the spectators and the marshals who do the shouting and the ducking.

Quiet, please

'Players should always show consideration for other players on the course and should not disturb their play by moving, talking or making unnecessary noise.'

'Players should ensure that any electronic device taken on the course should not distract other players.'

We've already covered the importance of silence and stillness and the adjunct is a clear reference to your mobile. If the R&A won't say it, you need to know that if you have to have a phone with you on the course, you'd be better off, and so would your companions, if you were back in the office. At the very least try to remember to switch it off or keep it on silent. Jabbering away on it incessantly or texting madly won't endear you to anyone and is unlikely to help your golf since you won't be concentrating.

Care of the course

The R&A are concerned about the care of the course but not nearly as much as the greenkeepers, committee and members of the club at which you are playing. They have put a lot of work, care, attention and money into the place and it behoves any visitors to treat it well and repair to the best of their ability any damage they do. Remember that you're not the only one playing the course and think how fed up you'd be if your ball ended up in a footprint or a Grand Canyon of a divot, so please:

- rake bunkers (or use a club to smooth out footprints)
- repair pitch marks on the greens
- repair scrapes made by your shoes before leaving the green
- replace divots on the fairways.

Raking or smoothing out the sand is easier if you take the shortest line into the bunker and walk out the same way, but use your head. Sometimes you have to take the long way round because of the nature of the terrain or the lie and jumping into a pot bunker is not recommended even for the young and lithe – if you don't get the ball out first time and it rolls back into your footprints, you're in even bigger trouble.

Greenkeepers are driven mad by unrepaired or badly repaired pitch marks because they take days to heal, so make it a habit to fix yours at once – and any others you may spot as you wait for your turn to putt. The little tools for repairing pitch marks come in a variety of shapes and sizes but all consist of two prongs so that you can gently raise the turf around the outside of the indentation, then tap it down with your putter. Some people use a tee for this but whatever your implement of choice, make sure you do a neat job and earn brownie points from the greenstaff.

You're allowed to repair pitch marks on the green that are on your line – that is, between your ball and the hole – but you're not allowed to tap down spike marks made by dragging your feet (or others dragging their feet) until after you've putted. Be particularly careful about where you're placing your feet near the hole.

Quite often you'll take a chunk out of the ground when you hit the ball and you must retrieve the bit of turf – the divot – and replace it, stamping it down firmly, so that the course repairs itself quickly and there's no hole for someone playing behind to end up in. Playing a ball out of a divot hole when you've driven down the middle of the fairway is very irritating and often not an easy shot. It will happen, of course, and sometimes the turf disintegrates and there's no divot, in which case you should tap the sides of the hole with your club and make it as neat as possible. At some courses you'll be asked to carry a small bucket of sand (with some seed in it) and use that to fill in your divots. (Strictly, the divot is the bit of turf but you'll often hear phrases of the 'I'm in a sodding divot' variety.)

Slow play

This is known in the book of rules as 'pace of play' but not many people nowadays seem to appreciate that golf is exercise and not an excuse for dawdling about taking an inordinate amount of time. Pace as understood by snails seems to have become the norm despite the strictures of the lawmakers.

'Players should play at a good pace... It is a group's responsibility to keep up with the group in front. If it loses a clear hole and it is delaying the group behind, it should invite the group behind to play through...'

Keeping up with the group in front is a crucial distinction from not holding up the group behind. The group behind may be having problems of their own and not be able to keep up with your group and may, indeed, be holding up the entire course. So long as you keep up with the group in front, you are doing all you can. If you are the group in front, the first people out, you set the pace and the aim should be not to hold anybody up because there is no doubt that slow play is the biggest problem facing the game today and turns many people off. How can I afford the time? I can't justify it. It takes too long. And so golf loses out and so do golfers because at its best, played at a brisk pace, the game has a rhythm and a flow to it that are lost in the start-stop-long-wait culture.

Once it used to be that two players would get round an 18-hole course in no more than two-and-a-half hours but that has now become more like three-and-a-half simply because people have not learned how to play quickly. It is commonplace for a fourball to take four-and-a-half to five hours for a round if the course is crowded.

It used to be the practice for clubs to sell daily green fees which meant that a fourball could play in the morning, have some lunch and play a second 18 in the afternoon. That still happens but increasingly golf is now sold by the round, given that there would not be enough daylight for some people to play twice in a day.

Slow play is a denial of the suggestion that 'individuals show consideration for other players' and to play excessively slowly is the most selfish thing a golfer can do. The way it works is that there is a certain amount of time allowable to play a hole, depending on the circumstances. If you are in a friendly fourball taking, say, three-and-a-half hours to get round, that works out at around 12 minutes per hole. But if one member of that group is taking ages over club selection, preparation to hit the shot, lining up the putt or simply walking slowly and lagging behind the others, then he is taking far too much of that 12 minutes. That in turn means that the three people he is playing with either have to hurry their own games or take as long as the slowcoach and fall behind on the golf course. An individual playing slowly is simply not being fair, either to those he is playing with or to the other people on the course who are being held up.

There are many slow players among the professionals, who like to consider a shot from every angle, taking into account every vagary, real, imagined or potential. They'll argue that it's their livelihood and there's a lot at stake, so precision is vital. Nick

Faldo and Bernhard Langer, for example, are painstakingly thorough and both have been timed frequently, with a view to fining them for falling behind but they are adept at speeding up when they know they have to – which is not quite the spirit that the R&A is looking for. Still, being a pragmatic bunch, they took precautions at one of their Open qualifying events and had the players graded from one to five by the European Tour officials who knew them best. The slowcoaches (the fives) were put out at the end of the field and there were very few disruptions.

Be ready

There are many very easy ways of avoiding being slow and the principal one of these is *always be ready when it is your turn to play*. This is astonishingly simple and yet almost no one observes it.

Let us say that you are playing a friendly fourball and that you are the third longest off the tee. Whoever is 'shorty' and first to play is allowed a reasonable amount of time to weigh up the shot and hit it but while he is doing that, you should also be working out what club you have to play and where you want to hit it. So many golfers just walk up to their ball and if it is not their turn, stand around with their minds in neutral, contemplating the trees, the birds or just their navels. Then, when it is their turn, and only then, do they start working out what they should be doing. That can easily waste a minute and if the remaining two members of the fourball do the same, that is three minutes wasted right there. Multiply this by 18 and it comes to an amazing 54 minutes that could be saved just by being ready.

There are other exceedingly easy ways of getting around a golf course without undue delay. You can, for instance, *walk* the course, rather than trudge or meander around it. That doesn't mean race round, just walk reasonably briskly – after all, part of the purpose of the game is to get some exercise.

Then there are the little tricks that come with experience. For instance, when walking up to the green, look for the path that leads to the next tee, so that you can put your bag down or park your trolley somewhere near it. (But don't even think of hauling your trolley across the green: that's sacrosanct. Remember, it's meant to be a smooth, pampered putting surface and even if it isn't, you should treat it as such, so that you automatically do the right thing when you're invited to play at Augusta.) If your ball is on the opposite side of the green to the path and you take your bag over there, the odds are that you will leave it there after putting and have to go back and retrieve it. Time wasted – and irritating for the people behind.

Be prepared to putt

Then there is the putting itself, and all that was said about being ready to play when it's your turn applies even more importantly on the green. When someone else is putting, use that time to survey your own putt so that when it is your turn, you know most of what you need to know and require only a last look and a couple of practice swings. The time taken by most people on the green is absurd and serves only to confuse.

When you have holed out, if you are marking a card, do not stand there on the green or next to it and enter your score. Walk briskly to the next tee and when the other members of your fourball are hitting off, use that time to keep the card up to date. Also, remember to have your driver or the club you're going to hit off the tee in your hand ready to play.

These tips are just some of the essentials that contribute to a fast-moving fourball but when you think about it, it is simple etiquette – sorry, good manners.

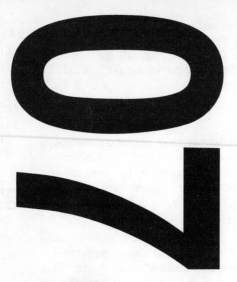

07

**learning
to score**

In this chapter you will learn:
• playing is more than swinging
• why course management matters
• to keep thinking.

> **Tip at the top**
>
> It's not how, it's how many.

A sweet swing is all very well but you don't get marks for style in golf: in the end it's the score that counts and the number of shots that you take, not the way that you make them. It all comes down to how many, not how.

Luther Blacklock, who has spent more than 30 years standing out in all weathers with thousands of pupils of all types, is passionate about helping players develop an effective swing and to this end he has invented a training device called Explanar®. 'Simply put,' says Luther, who is not surprisingly evangelical about his invention, 'it teaches golf in the way stabilisers teach people to ride bicycles. Learning balance is not acquired aurally, visually or intellectually. The same is true of golf. Albert Einstein and Lance Armstrong learnt to ride a bike the way most of us did – with dad holding the back of the saddle. We appropriated that skill by trial and error: it was felt, not taught. Explanar® turns golf swing theory into feelings, allowing the golfer to focus on executing the shot more effectively.

Control of the ball

It is absolutely essential to recognize from the beginning that you are going to learn how to hit golf shots and the varied skills that this entails. The object of golf is primarily to control the ball. It is a secondary consideration as to how you swing the club. Most golfers fail at golf by becoming bogged down with swing thoughts rather than focusing on creating the shot. Remember this advice from the outset: *It will be far more rewarding to shoot 76 with a slightly quirky swing than shoot 96 with a textbook swing.* Determine to become a shot-maker first and a swing-maker second.'

Hitting with a purpose

Most people get hooked on golf when they feel that first really good shot, the one that comes from the middle of the club face, climbs on the desired trajectory and goes an undreamed of distance, straight at the target. Eureka, we think, that was a great shot. It can be done. Then we have to learn that it doesn't happen every time and that there is a lot more involved when it comes to learning to score.

Some people see soaring drives as evidence that they are playing golf; for them length is not the best thing about the game, it is the only thing. We once played with a Japanese gentleman and were goggle-eyed when he hit his opening tee shot about 280 yards (256 m), dead straight. He made a bit of a mess of the second and third shots, and seemed to have little idea of how hard to hit a putt, but we put that down to the warming-up process. At the 2nd, a par four, he hit an immense drive that came to rest in a greenside bunker, more than 300 yards (274 m) away. Ah, now he's getting into his stride, we thought. But he never came out of that bunker. After about eight or nine ineffectual splashes with a wedge, he gave up and walked to the next tee. There he hit another big drive...but need we go on? It turned out that he had been playing golf for five years but this was only the third time he had been on a golf course.

To join a club in Japan was far beyond his means, so he became a 'driving range golfer' and one of the worst sort as well. All he ever did was beat balls as far as humanly possible and even though there were facilities for chipping and putting, and opportunities to hit all the iron shots, all he wanted to do was blast balls with his driver.

There is nothing wrong, of course, with being a good driver and if the golfer also has the gift of timing and hits it a long way, there is nothing wrong with that either. But prowess off the tee should never be at the expense of the remainder of the game.

The scrambler

To be a good short game player is just as admirable as to be a big hitter but this, it has to be admitted, is not a popular point of view. Even the top professionals hate to be thought of as 'scramblers', that is players who can rescue a round by being brilliant around the green. For the first few years of his stellar career, for instance, Nick Faldo was thought of as a magnificent

Tiger Woods (hitting with a purpose) – A force of nature. Incredibly gifted, the World No.1 hits the ball harder than almost anyone.

scrambler – and he hated it. He wanted to be known for the imperiousness of his long game. He was once asked what he wanted his legacy to be and he answered that he wanted people to say: 'Did you see Nick Faldo play?' You can be sure that by that he didn't mean: 'Did you see Nick Faldo hit that superb little chip at the 8th?'

That desire, to acquire a more glorious long game, was part of the reason he undertook a two-year re-working of his swing with David Leadbetter which, in combination with his still superb short game, led to the winning of six major championships and to people asking: 'Did you see Nick Faldo play?'

Play the percentages

Learning to score is absolutely basic and yet it is a skill that many people either cannot be bothered with or, in extreme cases, despise. It often means turning down a challenge that, as a beginner, you may succeed with once in a hundred goes – and those are not very good odds. Not many hardened gamblers would take a punt on a 100–1 shot. Yet often enough it is seen as unmanly not to go for the death-or-glory shot, in some way cowardly, for instance, to lay up short of the water.

Daly dunk

Some people get to the top of the game before they fully realize the importance of learning to score. John Daly has made a career of taking on the impossible and because of his outrageous talent sometimes succeeds. But not always. Once, in the Bay Hill Invitational event in Orlando, Florida, this double major champion hit his second shot at a par five into a lake that bordered the entire length of the hole. He took a penalty drop and, convinced he could reach the green, hit the same shot as before, with the same club, with the same result. He was beginning to lose his cool and he went on to whack a further seven balls into the water before walking off the hole with a score of 18!

Mickelson might

Phil Mickelson was an outstanding amateur golfer – he won a US Tour event before turning professional – and was tipped as the 'next Nicklaus'. But Mickelson not only loved the challenge of the extremely difficult shot, he even alleged that that was how he got his enjoyment from the game. He hit everything as hard

Nick Faldo (love to scramble) – Worked ferociously to make himself
technically perfect. Look and learn.

as he could and once boasted that Tiger Woods hated it when he smashed a drive past him. But while Woods was systematically winning major championship after major championship, Mickelson was finding ever more ways to lose them.

It was an unintelligent way to play the game but because of a God-given talent, Mickelson won ordinary tour events and made millions. Then, in the season of 2003, he began to slip and from always being in the top half dozen in the money list, he found himself down at number 38 and at long last realized he had to mend his ways. He spent the entire off-season with his coach, Rick Smith, working on a gentle fade off the tee and using a new, slightly softer ball. Those twin actions caused him to lose 20 or so yards (18 m) in distance off the tee but instead of often being in the trees or the rough he was now almost invariably on the fairway. He won two major championships in two years and said, apparently seriously, that he wished someone had pointed out the error of his previous ways a lot earlier. They had, of course, but he just hadn't listened.

Show or dough

There is an adage in golf that you drive for show but you putt for dough and it is not far from the truth. The dough is undoubtedly earned once you are relatively close to the green and in any case you use your putter a lot more during a round than you use your driver. If, as a beginner, you manage to get down in three shots from 100 yards (91 m) out every time, you won't be a beginner for long.

Beating balls as far as possible is great fun but if you want to score well, you're wasting your time going for more and more length. 'Wrong game plan,' says Peter Lane, an Advanced Professional who has spent his working life in Hertfordshire and is now at Harpenden. 'You can never win a game or a competition off the tee – but you can certainly lose it around the green. What people don't understand is that golf, at first, is not all about hitting greens in regulation and perfect play. It is understandable that they think it is because the media feeds us a diet of huge drives and brilliant shots. But these fantastic shots are delivered by only a tiny percentage of golfers, the top tournament professionals.

If you are going to learn how to score, you must understand that 70 per cent of all golf is played from within a range of 120 yards (110 m) or so from the hole. It doesn't matter how far you hit the ball off the tee if you cannot then get the ball on the green or aren't able to chip and putt successfully.

Work on these shots at the range. Find a club that you can hit comfortably 140 yards, a club that you feel happy with, that you know you can hit with confidence. Call it your comfortable club. It will be a great investment.'

First tee jazz

There is another adage in golf: the longest walk in the game is from the practice area to the first tee. It doesn't matter that they may be side by side, what the adage indicates is that it is difficult for the average human being to take what he or she has just been successfully practising and reproduce it on the first tee.

David Llewellyn, the Welsh National Coach suggests: 'The way to control those first-tee nerves – and we all get them – is not to think about technique. Even beginners should have a pre-shot routine by the time they get to the golf course because if you haven't got that, you're wasting your time. I like to focus on the pace of the swing, the rhythm, the tempo, call it what you like.

I always remember Ernie Els saying that the best advice he ever had was simply "1,2,3—4". That means counting "one, two three" to get to the top of the backswing and then "four" as you hit the ball. I won in Biarritz with that. I hadn't been playing very well and I was hopeless in practice and then I remembered that.

It needn't be figures. It could be "Fish-n—chips" or even, very simply, "back and—hit". Whatever you choose it should occupy your mind, allow you to focus on timing and not get confused with technique. It frees the muscles up to let you swing smoothly because no one can perform with tight muscles. If you need an illustration, stand up and consciously tighten all the muscles in your legs – you can't walk, can you? It's like that with the swing. Use that Viennese waltz if you like – da, da, da, da—dum – but don't stand there thinking about technique or you'll never hit the ball.'

Strategy

Lane has some straightforward thoughts on how to play the first hole. 'Try not to go to the first tee cold. Hit some practice balls if you can – most clubs have a net somewhere – and if this is possible focus on finding a rhythm that is comfortable for you. Tune in to your own swing DNA, the timing that suits you. If you can't hit balls even simple stretching exercises help.

Ernie Els (first tee jazz) – Watch him as much as you can to try and capture
the wonderful rhythm of his swing.

On the tee, assuming it's a par four, choose a club that you feel relatively happy with. It need not be a driver. A 3-wood, 5-wood or even an iron will do – who cares as long as you get it away? Next choose a club that will get you safely "into" the hole, not necessarily to the green – somewhere near will do. Then, if you've been working on that club on the range that will get you onto the green from 100 to 140 yards (91–128 m) out, here's where that practice pays off.

Some form of game plan is important so try to aim away from bunkers or water and do not try to hit the green with impossible shots. If you play for the green in three shots (or four or even more, depending on your expertise and the length and difficulty of the hole), you will find that a score of one over par (or even two over, sometimes even more) will be good enough almost every time, with the handicap shots that you get. Work out a realistic par for the hole for you and aim for what's likely not what's improbable.'

It is best to acknowledge – and even more important to accept – that no one can hit great shots on command. The best players the game has ever seen, the likes of Tiger Woods, Jack Nicklaus and Arnold Palmer all admit that if in a really good round of golf of, say, 66, they hit two or three great shots, then they are more than satisfied. They will have hit a great many *good* shots but there is a big difference between the two. They know that golf is such a capricious game that even they will never master it and that all the huge amounts of practice, all the psychological preparations, all the gym work, will never guarantee the hitting of a *great* shot. And their definition of what constitutes a great shot is rather different from that of a beginner.

The danger of expectations

The point is that even the best have no expectation of hitting a great shot, and if they haven't, why on earth would a beginner? But that is what happens. The beginner, standing over a shot that has to be hit 200 yards (182 m) to a green that has a stream running in front it, just knows he can do it – because he has. Once! The golfing mind can be a treacherous thing and it is prepared to forget the 99 failed attempts to make a 200-yard (182 m) carry on the driving range in favour of the solitary one that went the distance.

The result of attempting that carry, of going for the glory shot, is, more often than not, failure. Sometimes that failure is abject, as in when the ball is topped along the ground for a few bumbling yards; sometimes it is just about OK providing the ball stops short of the stream; and sometimes it is almost heroic as it plunges into the water. But once, just that once, it carries the hazard and finishes on the green and you have something to talk, no, to boast about for months. However, that shot should never be attempted, certainly not until the golfer is good enough at least to *know* that he can make the carry, that he can consistently hit the ball far enough through the air to get over the water. For most beginners that is still some way in the future.

So, faced with that shot, the fabled 200-yard (182 m) carry over water, what should be done? Well, the first thing to realize is that this is a game called golf not 'chicken'. It is not cowardly to avoid a challenge that you not only know, deep down, that you cannot achieve but that will also penalize you heavily on the scorecard. It is best to adopt an aspect of the game entitled, somewhat grandiosely, course management, something that for the beginner might be better called sensible play.

Recently one of us, playing that magnificent golf course at Brancaster, the Royal West Norfolk, was faced with just such a shot from only 180 yards (164 m) out. It was a foursomes match, which means that two partners hit alternate shots, and the tee shot lay on a fairway which ended about 90 yards (182 m) ahead, with marsh and sand from there to the elevated green. To reach the putting surface would have required an absolutely perfect shot and we calculated the chances of hitting such a blow as being slim at best and probably none. But if the second shot was hit just 90 yards (82 m), a relatively simple task, the third shot would also be only 90 yards (82 m), another relatively easy shot. So we did the sensible thing and were richly rewarded when that third shot rather luckily hit the pin, stopped 12 inches (30 cm) away and we got our par four. Had we attempted the second shot straight at the green the likelihood is that we would have found the marsh, had to take a penalty drop and still have had a difficult recovery shot to the green.

Course management, in the wrong hands, can simply be coarse management, with good, sensible thinking discarded for the chance of occasional – very occasional – glory. It is for that reason that any club professional would back him or herself to knock a dozen strokes off the average beginner's score without giving him or her a lesson or hitting a single ball. All the pro would have to do is walk around and nominate the shot to be played rather than leaving it to the beginner to decide. A large part of the advice would be the avoidance of obstacles through playing within your capabilities, taking the correct club for the most sensible shot and knowing where to aim, considering the difficulties ahead.

Use your head

It is not always best, for example, to take your driver off the tee at a long par five. There might be a bunker at the precise point where your best drive might finish, so take the 3-wood instead to be sure of being on grass, not in sand. Some holes feature cross-bunkers, sandy wastes that run all across the fairway and no one ever wants to go in one of those. (But we do of course, not being perfect and the road to par figures being paved with good intentions.) It is a certain shot dropped, if not two and if there is the slightest doubt about being able to carry such a hazard, play short. Ditto lakes and all water hazards.

Then there is the shot to the green. It is essential before playing the stroke to look and take notice of where the pin is. It only takes a glance but it can repay your foresight handsomely. If, for instance, the pin is on the left of the green and there is also a hazard, in the form of a bunker or some water, on the left, then do not aim for the pin itself, make a conscious effort to aim for the middle or the right-hand side of the green. That probably seems obvious but a great many golfers play the game all their lives without ever realizing the importance of playing away from danger. There's the pin, aim for it, they say.

The professionals, on the other hand, always know precisely which pin positions they feel they can attack in the hope of a birdie and which they know are too dangerous and have to be played away from. They call those the sucker pins.

At the top level, course management is all the things so far mentioned plus, occasionally, an element of tactics. For instance, in the US Open at Congressional in 1997 the championship came down to Ernie Els and Colin Montgomerie, level with each other on the last-but-one hole of the last round. It is a difficult par four, with a green surrounded by water and Els knew that whoever succeeded in getting a par was likely to have the advantage. So, cleverly, he hit a 3-wood off the tee, while Montgomerie hit a driver. They were both good shots but Els's was, naturally, shorter than the Scot's and so Els had to play first. In golf, once you've played from the tee, it's the person furthest from the hole who plays first. That was precisely what he wanted, because he was backing himself to hit another good shot onto the green and put added pressure on to his opponent. And that is precisely what happened. The South African hit a superb shot which finished around 12 feet (3.6 m) from the hole and Montgomerie, conscious that he now must answer that challenge, failed to do so, took three putts and lost the championship by one shot.

The caddie

Sometimes it is down to the professional caddies to recognize when a bit of course management is needed and their advice, if offered at the right time, in the right way, can be hugely influential. For instance, in the 1986 Open Championship at Turnberry, Greg Norman was attempting to win his first major title, after years of under-achievement, and was going well until he got to the 7th tee.

Suddenly he hit a horrible drive, curving low and left – a shot called a 'duck hook' in the game. It finished in deep rough and as Norman and his caddie, Pete Bender, left the tee to go to find the ball, the latter said: 'Greg, you're going too fast.' By that he meant Norman was doing everything too fast, walking, thinking and swinging but all he got in acknowledgement from the Australian was a distracted, 'Yeah, yeah.' Bender, who knew not only that he was right but also how important it was that his man slow everything down, grabbed hold of Norman's sweater and said again, very deliberately: 'You-are-going-too-fast.'

This time it sank in. Norman realized that his concentration had slipped, took notice of what Bender had said and went on to win that championship by five shots.

Muzzy magic

Another great caddie effort came in 1988 at the Augusta National golf club where Sandy Lyle was trying to win the Masters. Lyle had led after 36 and 54 holes and throughout the final round as well until he got to the short 12th, a notoriously difficult par three, where he dumped his tee shot into Rae's Creek, the water in front of the green. He had to take a penalty drop with the water still in front of him and ended up taking five, a double bogey, to lose his lead to Mark Calcavecchia. 'I've lost it now,' was Lyle's rather despondent reaction but Dave Musgrove, his caddie of many years, spoke up.

'Nonsense,' he said, 'we've had the lead long enough. Let someone else suffer for a bit. We'll get it back later.' Which is what happened. Lyle, reassured by the words of a man who was a good friend as well as a great caddie, went on to birdie the last hole of the tournament, to win by one.

Course management, then, comes in many forms – from the player himself, from a watching professional or from a good caddie. But essentially it all boils down to the same thing: just think sensibly. And never forget to have fun. That should be easier for those of us who are not involved in the white heat of holing putts to earn millions but even we can sometimes lose the plot.

Lane's wise words

'Golf is a game where you need to focus on what you are doing, not on what you perhaps should be doing. So take five minutes before playing to write down, on paper, all the things that may be bothering you – the job, family, friends, the car, anything you can think of. Put the paper in your golf bag and forget the problems. You can deal with them when you get off the course because you are safe in the knowledge that you have your reminder.

Also, try to be calm and enjoy playing, no matter how poorly. Everyone knows someone who would love to be playing golf, no matter how bad, but cannot. My father was golf mad and loved the experience of just playing, no matter how badly. He died suddenly and when things are not going my way on the course and I maybe get a little upset, I just think of Dad and how he would have loved to be here, no matter how bad his play. And that makes two of us.'

08

getting more serious

In this chapter you will learn:
- how to beat Tiger
- a bit about handicaps
- how to control your temper.

Tip at the top

How do you write a nine?

Dr Kitrina Douglas was a British amateur champion, won ten tournaments as a professional, represented Europe in their first winning Solheim Cup team at Dalmahoy and now has more degrees and doctorates than you could shake a 7-iron at. In partnership with Dr David Carless, she has planned, developed, researched and written a total of seven coach education sections or training manuals for the PGA. She has worked with golfers with learning difficulties and mental health problems, with beginners and professionals, male and female. Her book, *100 Tips for Lady Golfers*, is full of useful, useable information that all golfers, not just women, should find helpful. Kitrina's worth listening to and she's always learning.

'When I started playing golf, I knew that there would probably be a difficult and an easy way to learn. I therefore had lessons every week and in three years my handicap came down from 36 to 14, 14 to three, three to one. I remember one of the ladies from my club asking me to play a few holes and when I explained that I didn't have time because I was going for a lesson, she exclaimed, "Oh, haven't you learnt yet?"

I hope I never stop learning. Golf is such a fascinating yet fun game that I am continually learning new shots and gaining a better understanding of the game. Whatever your standard, don't restrict your learning, make the most of it.

Look and learn

The most important lesson I learned in golf was something I discovered for myself when I was a 14-handicap golfer who had been playing for less than a year. After watching the world No. 1 woman golfer, Nancy Lopez, on television one afternoon I went to the club and played five holes. On the tee, so fresh in my memory was Nancy's swing that I almost imagined I was Nancy. Although an onlooker might suggest she and I swing differently, in my senses I felt as if I had her poise and rhythm.

I went on to have the best five holes of my golf career up to that date. As a mid-handicap player I was not expecting nor expected to score so low and yet I did. In my mind, without a doubt, that afternoon's play was made possible because I had been watching someone with a good swing on television and consequently, without thinking, had subconsciously mimicked her rhythm. During the five holes I had also become aware of how good rhythm would affect the technical aspects of my swing. I became aware that my swing felt as if I could repeat it all the time because it felt so easy, rhythmical and natural.

As I became a better player and then turned professional I found it helpful to take a video of my favourite player with me as I travelled to play in tournaments. Simply by watching the video for five minutes, especially as the pressure mounted, I found it restored an elusive feel for a correct movement without having a lesson or being over-concerned with technique.

The simple tip is to watch and become aware. Try spending a few moments just looking at a swing that appeals to you (preferably someone with similar body shape and size to you); try to get a clear picture of the tempo of their swing in your mind; close your eyes and play the swing in your mind like you would a video. If you can video a few of the swings of your favourite player all the better but don't just watch, try and gain some awareness in your body for the movement as well.

By watch and become aware I do not mean analyse it. The golf swing can easily become overcomplicated when we analyse every movement and try working out "what went wrong". Unfortunately as adults we become accustomed to taking instruction in verbal queues. As infants most of us learned to walk before we could understand instruction and most of us perfected crawling, walking and running without continual lessons. Why? Because we watched and simply allowed ourselves a chance to become self-aware.

Remember, on the course it's counterproductive to be thinking about technique, about how to swing the club. Think instead about rhythm and playing the game.'

Handicaps

Kitrina mentioned that mysterious word handicap but it's not that mysterious really and it's the key to the inclusivity of golf, the reason why boys and girls, men and women, professionals and amateurs can all play together – even in the same competition. Handicaps make it possible, not just in theory, for, say, a 14-year-old girl to beat Tiger Woods and for a pensioner, with the right amount of handicap strokes (and some judicious negotiating), to beat Ernie Els.

Some people play all their lives without an official handicap and have no interest in acquiring one but if you ever want to play in competitions, you will need one. It indicates a level of competence. The lower your handicap the better player you are. Some very good amateurs have a plus handicap, which means that they have to add their handicap to their score whereas the rest of us subtract ours from our total (or gross) score.

To obtain a handicap you have to submit a number of scorecards (usually three), each attested by your playing partner, preferably someone with a handicap. You will be allocated a handicap on the basis of your scores, with the maximum allowed for a man being 28 and the maximum for a woman 36. Juniors can go up to 54 but once they're good enough, they come under the same system as adults.

The individual national golf unions are responsible for their country's handicapping system and most clubs have a handicap secretary but every player is responsible for making sure that he or she plays off the correct handicap. Professionals, who make their living from the game, do not have handicaps as a general rule but amateurs do. The Rules of Amateur Status are laid out in *The Rules of Golf* but in essence an amateur is someone who doesn't get paid for playing the game.

Getting a handicap is the key to flying with your fledgling game all round the world of golf. Get a handicap and you can play those courses that refuse to allow non-handicap golfers on their premises. And just how do you get a handicap? Well, by playing at those self-same courses that won't let you play without a handicap. Many clubs will say that you can't play their course until you've got a handicap and when you ask them how you can get a handicap without playing the course that's just refused you, the response is a shrug of the shoulders. It is at this point, the classic Catch 22 situation, that some, understandably, despair and wander off into the ungolfing darkness.

Don't. Help is at hand. The English Golf Union (EGU) have recognized that there is a practical problem here, one that puts would-be golfers and golf club members off and turns them away from the game. This is not at all what the EGU – or, to be fair, the clubs themselves – wants. If the game is to grow and if these islands are to prosper at the top levels of the game, more people must be attracted into it and it is part of the responsibility of the home unions (in England, Ireland, Scotland and Wales) to encourage such growth.

The EGU, for instance, has set up a section called the Associate Membership Programme, which is open to anyone. All you have to do is go to their website (see Taking it further at the end of the book) and click on 'Not a club member' and you are directed to a section that will help you not just get a handicap but also find clubs in your area that have vacancies for men, women, boys or girls. The website is full of helpful advice and stresses: 'Members of the Associate Membership Programme receive an official EGU or English Ladies' Golf Association (ELGA) handicap, allowing them to play courses around the world. It is designed to encourage golfers of all standards, ages and genders to get into golf and to enjoy the game. It encourages improvement of your playing ability through a desire to lower your handicap and it allows you to play a friendly round with like-minded golfers.'

It costs just £40 – no more than a ticket for a single Premiership football match that lasts 90 minutes. Compare that with what you are buying into when you get a handicap: a lifetime of golf and good sport.

Also, with your membership comes a goodie bag which, among other things, contains three Titleist (say title-ist quickly) golf balls which alone are worth around £7. You can either join through the website or by getting in touch with the EGU or ELGA.

You will be asked to complete a written rules and etiquette assessment and also return to them three cards, properly filled in and signed by a playing partner and a handicap will then be assessed. You will also be asked to keep that handicap current – as you would at a golf club – by recording the score of every round you play and sending it to the EGU.

Beware the bandit

This last requirement is actually for your protection. As a beginner, reading the invaluable advice and tips given in this book, practising them and taking lessons from PGA professionals, it is likely that your game will be improving rapidly. If this is the case then your scores will be coming down just as quickly and so should your handicap. But there is a word for those whose game improves but their handicap remains the same – 'bandit' – and it is a word that you should never want to be applied seriously to you. In golfing terminology it means someone who is deliberately playing off a higher handicap than his ability warrants, in order to take the money, to win matches and competitions. It is sometimes used light-heartedly but when it gets serious, it is no laughing matter.

A real bandit is the worst form of cheat, in that the cheating is premeditated and has started before he or she actually gets to the golf course. If you say your handicap is 24 and you then play a course that has a par of 72 (the target score for a player playing off nought or zero, known as scratch) in a total of 84 shots, then you have played to 12, which is 12 shots better than your handicap. While that may happen very occasionally as a one-off, if it happens two or three times, unpleasant conclusions begin to be drawn.

Having a handicap is a wonderful thing: you are not a proper golfer until you have one. But for the sake of your reputation and thus your whole future in the game, you have to be sure it is honestly obtained and honestly maintained.

We have a friend who is a fine golfer and in every respect a good companion, one of the first you would invite to share your dinner table. But he has this overwhelming compulsion that he must win at golf and while he simply would not dream of, say, moving his ball in the rough, he has for years insisted that his handicap is just in double figures. In fact, he is rarely more than three or four over par, which results in two things. One, his compulsion is usually satisfied and he wins, and two, no one, but no one, will play him for money.

The idea of a handicap, of course, is that everyone – in theory at least – starts equal on the first tee and the match or competition will be determined on form, by who happens to be playing the best that day. No one wants to stand on that first tee knowing that someone else, because they have a false handicap, has won before the thing has started. Having a handicap should mean being able to play against anyone, literally, and have a chance of beating them – even if you are a 14-handicapper at your club and your opponent is the world No. 1 Tiger Woods.

Making your own luck

In a famous, or perhaps infamous, match at the Limerick golf club, in Ireland, in 2001, local member J. P. McManus actually did take on Woods, and not only beat him, he thrashed him – by the massive margin of 5 and 4 – five up and four to play. In fact at the end of the match Woods said, albeit with a big smile on his face: 'I will continue to play competitively – but as far as J. P. is concerned, I'm in retirement.'

McManus is a multi-multi millionaire who used to have a share in Manchester United and is a financier and gambler of some expertise. Along the way he has become friends with Woods, who comes over to Ireland, usually before an Open Championship, to relax, play in a charity pro-am and get in some links golf before the big test the following week. He was doing this when McManus challenged him to a head-to-head confrontation, with the aid of his handicap strokes.

Special rules

McManus hasn't made his millions without knowing something about odds and he knew that even getting 14 shots would probably not be enough, so he devised a set of handicap rules to suit the situation. He decided that both he and Woods would hit each shot twice: two shots off the tee, two shots from the fairway and so on, right down to taking each putt twice. The cunning plan was that McManus would be able to take his best effort and Woods had to take the worst of his, with McManus having the final say in that matter. If McManus hit one drive into the trees and the other in the fairway, he could take the ball in the fairway but if Woods did the same he had to take the ball in the trees.

Where this unique arrangement probably counted most against Woods was actually on the green. For instance, on the 7th hole, a difficult par four, McManus looked like losing it when, after two shots, he was still short of the green and Woods was only nine feet from the pin. The Irishman transformed the situation with a wonderful pitch shot to a few inches and so got his par four which, with his handicap stroke, became a nett birdie three. Woods then holed his putt also for a birdie three – but, of course, it didn't count. He had to take the putt again and this time he missed it. So he lost a hole he had looked like winning and, under normal arrangements, would have halved. By winning that hole McManus went four up and not even Woods, operating under these abnormal handicapping arrangements, could get back from there.

The *Irish Examiner* (and we're indebted to their golf man Charlie Mulqueen for the copious details) ran reports of the match on their front page, headlined: 'Gambler JP gives Tiger a lesson on winning' and in the sports section the headline was: 'The great Tiger is tamed by local hero JP in lopsided encounter.' Great stuff.

So get a handicap, join a club, play with friends and other club members, in matches and competitions and do so from a mark that truly reflects your ability.

Marking a card

At first sight it would seem that nothing could be simpler than marking a scorecard in golf. After all, what is it but putting down a few figures on a piece of cardboard? The tongue in cheek tip at the top of this chapter recalls a *Peanuts* cartoon in which The Masked Marvel, alias Snoopy, is designated to write down the scores. 'We all got nines on the first hole,' he's told and he looks at the card, pencil in paw, in puzzlement, thinking, 'How do you write a nine?'

The first thing to do is to learn how to read a scorecard. From left to right you will find several columns, how many depends on the complexity of the card, which in turn is determined by the golf club that designed and produced it. The column furthest left will usually (but not always) be reserved for the marker's score, and that is you. In golf you always record the score of a fellow competitor but the marker's column is for you to have a note of your own score, which is important because you're responsible for your own score and you will have to check your card against your opponent's at the end of the round.

The next column will have the number of the hole, from 1 to 18; there may be a column for the name of the hole; and then there will be a column with the length of each hole, either in yards or metres (there will be more than one of these, depending on which tees you play from). The next column will usually have the par of the hole – the number of strokes an expert player is expected to take – and this will be followed by the stroke index column. This indicates where handicap strokes should be taken in match play. If you have a handicap of 18, you will get a stroke at every hole. If your handicap has come down to, say, 12, then you will get a stroke at the holes where the index is from 1 to 12 but if you are just starting and have a higher handicap of, say, 28, then you will get one stroke at holes with an index of 1 to 18 and two strokes at holes 1 to 10. If your handicap is 36, you get two strokes at every hole.

The next column will be the 'player' column and this is where you put down the scores for the player whose round you are recording, not your own scores which, it must be said again, go in the marker column. There are numerous variations on this theme but you'll learn to pick out the important things: the number of the hole, the length of the hole, the yardage, the stroke index, your score and the score of the player whose card you are marking – and where you sign the card.

Once the round is over, check the two cards carefully (your own and that of the player you marked for) – the easiest way is for you to read the score for each hole out to each other. If this is a medal play competition (one that is won on a basis of the total number of strokes taken) then the scores for each hole are added together and the total is known as the gross score. When the handicap is then taken away from that total, we have the nett (or net) score – and at most clubs there are usually prizes for both. If you have a handicap of 20, the par of the course is 72 and you go round in 92, you have played to your handicap.

Finally, do not forget to sign the card. At the bottom of the card there will be a space for the marker's signature and another for the player's signature and it is your responsibility to ensure that you have signed in the marker's space for the player whose card you have marked and then in the player's space for your own card. (Your name should also be at the top of your card.)

Only then should the cards be handed in to the committee running the competition. If they are handed in without a signature, disqualification can result and if they are handed in with a wrong score recorded anywhere, that too can bring about disqualification. (The addition is the responsibility of the committee.)

Harrington horror

It sounds simple and it is. But some famous and hugely experienced professionals have been caught out, either through a wrong score being written down for a hole, or for not signing the card in the right place. Take Padraig Harrington, for instance. In the 2000 Benson and Hedges tournament at The Belfry, he had a brilliant third round and was leading comfortably with only 18 of the 72 holes left to play. The Belfry hotel decided that they would like to frame all the cards and put them on one of their walls but consternation followed when they discovered that Harrington had not signed his first round card. There were two signatures on it but neither was Harrington's. His marker Jamie Spence has signed it, but so too had the third member of the group, Michael Campbell (US Open champion in 2005). It was completely inadvertent, an accidental mix-up that, amazingly, went unspotted by the players and the recorders, who, in professional golf, are there to prevent just such a thing happening.

Harrington had to be disqualified because, regardless of the circumstances, he had not actually signed the card and it cost him the chance to win the tournament and the first prize of £166,600.

De Vicenzo oversight

Roberto de Vicenzo, the genial Argentine who won the Open in 1967 at Hoylake, might also have won the Masters at Augusta the following year but for a mistake by his marker (and himself). In the final round of the championship de Vicenzo had a birdie three at the 17th, seen by millions on television, and if it had been recorded properly, his score would have tied that of the American Bob Goalby.

However, de Vicenzo's marker, Tommy Aaron, in a lapse of concentration, wrote down a par four at the 17th and the Argentine failed to notice and signed his card. Then, as now, the higher score had to stand, so instead of tying with Goalby and going into a play-off, de Vicenzo came second. 'What a stupid I am', he said cheerfully. (If he had signed for a lower score than he had taken, he would have been disqualified.) He never won another major championship.

Simple though cardmarking is, it is important to get it right.

Marking the ball

For the most part in golf the ball must be played as it lies, which means that apart from exceptional circumstances dictated by whoever is running the competition (or winter rules), you must not touch the ball from the moment you hit it from the tee to the moment you hit it onto the green. Only on the putting surface are you permitted to lift, clean and replace your ball, on the understanding that after lifting and cleaning it, you replace it *exactly* on the same spot from which it was picked up. This means the ball goes back onto the same blade of grass from which it was lifted, and if you do otherwise, you are cheating.

The ball marker is usually a small, round, flat piece of plastic or metal with a prong underneath that can be pressed into the turf to ensure that the marker does not move. This should be placed very precisely behind the ball before it is picked up and, if necessary, cleaned.

It need not be one of these mass-produced markers. Many tournament professionals use a small coin which they slide underneath the ball, often a 'lucky' coin given to them by family or friends. But the principle is the same. Do not replace the ball even fractionally ahead of the marker because this is not allowed.

Woosie's woe

One famous golfer once broke all the rules for marking your ball on the green, without thinking. Ian Woosnam was playing for Wales in the 1991 World Cup in Rome and had hit his ball onto the green. The trouble was that he was bursting to go to the loo and knew that there was a portable toilet at the back of the green. So he marched onto the green, picked up his ball and marched off to the loo – completely forgetting to put down a marker at all. Then, of course, he marched back onto the green and, to the general amusement of the crowds, starting looking around for his non-existent marker. His playing partners had simply assumed that when he picked up his ball he had marked it, so they couldn't help, and it took shouts from the crowd to bring the sad, bad news to the Welshman that he was going to be penalized, in this case by one shot.

At a European Tour event in Cannes, in southern France, two of the competitors refused to sign the card of a third, alleging that he repeatedly put his ball back too far in front of his marker. The accused player at first denied it and then when it became clear that his playing partners were not going to be moved, said words to the effect that perhaps he had put the ball back a few millimetres in front of the marker but, as he said: 'On a 40-metre putt, 'how can that help?'

In practical terms, it couldn't help but as every gambler knows, if you *think* you've got an edge, you *have* got an edge and that is what he was trying to gain. His, though, was a non-existent edge: he was disqualified and within a season was off the tour.

Cheating

There is no sport in the world at which it is easier to cheat and also no sport in the world where it is more self-defeating. There is no umpire or referee to police your game so you are on your honour not to cheat and if you do so, it is your own honour that is besmirched. That's a very old-fashioned phrase but it's non-negotiable. Cheating is the cardinal sin in golf. There's no denying that people do cheat at golf for all the usual reasons – fear, greed, glory, gain, whatever – but if you are ever caught cheating in golf, you will forever be known as a cheat, and no amount of protestation will help. If you're a member of a club, you may or may not be drummed out – the probability is that you will – but even if you stay, you will be a pariah, no one will want to play with you.

For what is the point of playing with a cheat? If you know he or she is prepared to break the rules in order to win, what chance have you got? What satisfaction can a cheat get from winning, knowing that he has done so unfairly? If you think that athletes, like the Canadian sprinter Ben Johnson who won, and was then disqualified from the Olympics 100 metres sprint final for drug taking, are disgraced, that is as nothing compared to a club golfer caught moving his ball in the rough, or losing the ability to count correctly.

The fact is that it is the simplest thing in the world to move your ball just fractionally in the rough and suddenly you have a good lie instead of a bad one and that can make a two to three shot difference to your score on the hole. If you hit your ball in the trees and your partner/s are elsewhere, it is simplicity itself to move it from behind a trunk to beside it, and so have a shot back to the fairway.

It is easy, too, to 'forget' that duffed shot behind the bushes that no one saw, and say, airily, when asked your score: 'Oh, six,' when it was seven or eight. But be warned. You will only do it until the occasion you are found out and then it is goodbye golf.

Presidential privilege

Cheats come from all walks of life and Sam Snead, winner of seven major championships and one of the game's all-time greats, went to his grave insisting that Richard Milhous Nixon – 'Tricky Dicky' – President of the United States, was a golfing cheat. They played together at The Greenbrier in White Sulphur

Springs, a resort at which Snead was the professional emeritus and where he knew every inch of the property. Nixon, at one hole, hit his ball into scrub so dense that Snead knew two things, one that the ball would never be found and two, if it was, there was no room to swing a club anyway. That being the case Snead did not even bother going to look for the ball and was astonished when it came flying out of the jungle and onto the fairway. 'I know he threw it,' said Snead ever thereafter, 'but what could I say? He was the President.'

More practicalities

On a more pleasant note, once you have learned to hit the ball in reasonably consistent fashion, in the air and fairly straight, it will be exceedingly helpful to you to know how far you hit each of your clubs. This is not for bragging purposes, for long hitters are like those gunmen in the western films: just as there was always someone faster to the draw, there will always be someone longer than you.

You need to know how far on average you hit not just your driver but all the other clubs, the better to navigate your way round the golf course. There are rough rules of thumb for the distance you can get with each of your irons, for instance, a well-struck 7-iron will go around 140 yards (128 m). But generalized figures are next to useless. Some people will be lucky to get 120 yards (110 m) once in a while with a 7-iron and others may pump it 160 yards (146 m) or more every time.

Jack Nicklaus used to hit 50 shots, select the middle 15 and gauge his average length from that. There are lots of computerized gizmos that could help you measure distances now but the easiest course of action is to go to the practice ground with some decent balls and sort it out for yourself. Take a friend and make it a bit of fun, not a chore. If you go to the driving range, beware the balls: in general they're too soft to be much use for this exercise. The knowledge you acquire will be priceless and you will need it at all stages of a round of golf.

Yardage books

This knowledge is best used in conjunction with a helpful little booklet that most courses now sell in the professional's shop. It usually contains an overall plan of the course and has a diagram of each hole with the yardage between certain recognizable points being clearly marked on the map. Let us say that a particular hole has a fairway bunker meant to catch errant tee shots, a large oak in front of the green that has to be avoided, a stream just past the tree and then a bunker short of the green and another one behind it. The booklets – often called strokesavers after the company (Strokesaver®) that produces many of them – will give you a measurement between tee and bunker; from bunker to both tree and stream; and then, to the bunkers fore and aft. There will probably be more measurements of, say, a copse, a bunch of bushes, a depression in the fairway, a greenkeeper's hut – anything that helps the golfer judge just how far there still is to go. The booklets are not free but they are worthwhile because most people's eyes, when it comes to judging distance, are faulty.

Indeed part of the golf course architect's craft is to try to fool golfers with the concept of 'dead' ground. This can be done by creating a dip in the surface just before the green, so that the eye runs over it without adding that ground into the calculations or by placing a bunker in such a way that it appears to be nestling by the green when in fact it is 40 or so yards (36 m) in front of it. In both instances the deceived golfer will hit what he/she regards as a satisfactory shot, only to see that he/she should have hit another, much longer, club. That, of course, won't happen if, by consulting the booklet, you *know* you are 170 yards (155 m) away when it only looks like 140 (128 m).

Calculating distance

The idea of taking measurements is relatively new, coming into the game in the early 1960s when it was popularized by Nicklaus. He nicked the idea from Deane Beman, a good player who later became the commissioner for the US Tour, who in turn nicked it from a good amateur golfer called Gene Andrews.

At the time, the convention was that everything was done on eyesight and instinct, in other words, an educated guess. Andrews guessed wrong too many times and had the idea of mapping golf holes and measuring the various distances. The resulting sketches were so popular he started selling them to friends and fellow competitors. He said: 'Feel takes up so much time and effort to develop and then you lay off for a couple of weeks and you've lost it. So all my life I've been trying to get away from relying on it.'

Beman picked up on the idea, and told his good friend Nicklaus about it at the 1961 US Amateur Championship at the exposed Pebble Beach course on the coast of California. In his book, *My Story*, Nicklaus recalls: 'In practice rounds the blustery Pacific winds combined with firm fairways and greens had been giving me fits on approach shot yardages. When I mentioned the problem to Deane he said: "Why don't you measure them, like me?" Savvy little Deane, as Gene Andrews had been doing for years, had ingrained the habit of pacing off and noting down yardages, while I and almost everyone else in the amateur game continued to rely on visual estimating. I found that the more yardages I paced off, the more greens I hit and the closer I got to the pins.' Nicklaus won the championship.

More technology

Since then most good courses around the world have acquired yardage charts and no top golfer would be without his own, customized version. In 2005 they were still the best and cheapest way of finding out just what club is needed for the shot in question but this was also the year that the R&A relaxed the rules on GPS systems – the Global Positioning Satellite system that can pinpoint to the inch how far away a given object is.

GPS systems have been popular for a few years in America, particularly at resort courses, where they are commonly affixed to the golf carts or buggies in which players ride around these courses. The precise distance you are from your selected target appears on a screen, so that even the relatively easy task of working out your yardage from a booklet is not necessary. Up until 2005 these gadgets were illegal in any form of competition, but rather surprisingly the R&A changed its mind and ruled that the committee running the competition, be it amateur or professional, had the right to allow, or disallow them.

It may not be too long before we all know, to the millimetre, how far we have to hit our next shot but whether we will then be able to do it remains the trick.

Morris's mental magic

A big part of being a good golfer is being able to control yourself not just your ball and Karl Morris considers golf a good opportunity to develop and practise mental skills that will assist you in other areas of your life, be it family, business or other hobbies.

He says: 'I think that the reason that we love golf so much is that it provides the ultimate physical and mental challenge. Talented athletes from other sports, like Michael Jordan from basketball or David Beckham from soccer, display almost complete mastery in their own game but are transfixed by the unending challenge of the game with the little white ball and the small hole. Because the game is such a physical and mental challenge it makes sense that right from the word go you need to work not only on your physical development but your mental strength too.

Wouldn't it be useful to develop more focused concentration; or the ability to bounce back after disappointment or setback; or the skill of developing true self-confidence and having a greater understanding of how to control your moods amidst the inevitable ups and downs of life?

Just imagine if golf became some kind of laboratory where you were able to look at some areas of your life where fear is stopping you from moving forwards towards what you truly want from life and that through the game of golf you gained a greater understanding of what makes you really tick so that you could overcome some of those self-imposed limitations. Wouldn't that be a game worth playing?

Anger management

Anger is the big one for most people in terms of attitude or what I call *state control* (controlling your state). Is there any game in the world likely to push your buttons in the way that golf does? The big problem is not so much the shot that you have just hit badly, not even the fact that you have got really angry: it is how long that anger lasts and how long it stays in your system and the effect on your game over the next few holes.

When you get angry, the emotional part of your brain is put on full alert and this part of your brain doesn't think it *just reacts*. Think of this as the cave man within. When this guy is out of the cave, he really wants to run away very quickly or stand and fight, which is a great reaction if you're faced with a sabre-toothed tiger but not so great if you're trying to hole a sliding left-to-right putt.

Wonderful golfing attributes like rhythm, feel and touch go out of the window and the really big problem is that when cave man is out of his cage, he will not go straight back in. If you get really angry on one hole, your system will be out of kilter for a good while. How often do you see a card ruined by an outburst of anger followed by a string of bogeys (or worse)?

Managing anger and the emotional brain is a key mental skill. It may also help the rest of your life too.

Clear the air

We all buy into the idea that we can fly into a rage. Well, how about the concept of flying into a calm? The principle is the same. We just need to know how to trigger calm.

Probably the most effective anger management tool I have come across is called the "clear the air breath". Imagine that after you hit your shot you are going to walk ten paces and at that point you exhale all the air in your lungs. You literally clear the air and as you do this the shot is over, done, finished. You may wish to do as many of the tour players I work with do and actually say: "Done."

To be really angry we have to be breathing in a certain way, high and shallow in the chest. So as you clear the air you clear the way to get your game back on track.'

09

coping with hazards

In this chapter you will learn:
- how to play out of bunkers
- how to play over bunkers
- to have no fear.

Tip at the top

Golf was never meant to be fair.

Golf is an outdoor game played over diverse terrain so it is inevitable that you will find yourself in trouble from time to time, no matter how good you become. The trick is to accept it as part of the game and extricate yourself as efficiently as possible in the fewest number of strokes. As you progress you'll learn what you yourself are capable of: what shots you can attempt and what shots are beyond you. Get out of trouble as soon as you can and leave the attempted heroics to others (as a general rule). In some circumstances you'll be unable to play a shot at all and will have to declare the ball unplayable and take what's known as a penalty drop, adding a stroke to your score. It's nothing to be ashamed of and is frequently a better bet than hacking away getting cross and going nowhere.

Bunkers

We're going to start with bunkers because many beginners are petrified of bunkers. They are petrified of being in them because they feel that they are not going to get out and they are petrified of being behind one because they feel that very shortly they are going to be in it – and unable to get out. Every player who over the years has learned a degree of competency at the game can recall the days when bunkers represented an impossible obstacle and because you knew you couldn't get out it became a self-fulfilling prophecy that you went in.

Lawrence's lesson

'That's where sports psychology has done a really good job,' says Lawrence Farmer, an Advanced Fellow of the PGA, long-time professional at Moor Park in Hertfordshire and one of the best and most congenial of coaches. 'The power of positive thinking can work wonders – providing you've had the practical lesson first. Always remember that the good players would usually prefer to be in the sand rather than in the rough because they have mastered the bunker shot and can play it with more precision from a good lie than a shot from out of the grass.

The bunker shot is the only shot in golf where you don't hit the ball. You have to hit the sand before the ball and you have to commit to hitting it because if you quit on it, the sand will stop the club and the ball will go nowhere.

To practise this, I like to put a ball in a bunker and draw a circle around it about two to three inches away and then just try to remove that area of sand. The ball will go with it of course, out onto the green. It's no good scooping at the ball. You have to realize that the reason the ball goes up in the air is because you are hitting down on it and the loft of the club does the rest.

Here is a very effective drill for getting the feel of what should be happening when you play a proper shot out of the sand. In a practice bunker place a short piece of planking on top of the sand and then just swing at it with your sand wedge a few times. The club will just bounce off the surface of the wood but when you hit the piece of wood, the club will naturally carry on into a good follow-through and this is something you should try to achieve when playing a regular bunker shot.'

L

T

figure 9.1 a sand iron – note the leading edge 'L' is higher than the trailing edge 'T'

Tool of the trade

The sand iron, with its broad sole or flange, was invented by Gene Sarazen in the 1930s and makes escaping from bunkers less of a lottery, so learn to love it and it will repay your devotion in shots saved. **NB** You are not allowed to ground your club – that is, rest the club on the ground – in a bunker. The club is not allowed to touch the sand before you hit the ball and if it does, you are penalized two strokes in stroke play and lose the hole in match play. This restriction does not apply, fairly enough, to blind golfers.

Good lies

Lawrence's lesson applies if you have a good lie in the bunker and can play the type of recovery that is called a splash shot – or an explosion shot – out of the sand. A good lie is when the ball is lying cleanly on top of sand that has a bit of give in it, sand that is soft and yielding: not sand that is hard-packed, for instance, as sometimes happens after rain or in winter conditions.

The key to the shot, as is so often the case, is all in the address position – how you set up to the ball – and in the way you position the clubhead behind the ball. You'll see from the illustration (Figure 9.1) that your sand iron has two edges to it: the leading edge and the trailing edge, which is what we're concentrating on for the splash shot. The trailing edge is what enables the clubhead to slide underneath the ball and remove it from the bunker with a sliver of sand (imagine the whole lot looking like an impeccably fried egg).

Dial a recovery

The easiest way to make sure that the trailing edge hits the sand first is to get yourself organized outside the bunker, bearing in mind that once you're in the bunker you have to keep the clubhead hovering above the sand. Before taking your grip, place the club on the ground with the face square – the standard position – and imagine that you're looking down at the face of a clock. Turn – or dial – the leading edge slightly to the right, so that it is now pointing to one o'clock instead of 12 o'clock. The shaft of the club is more or less straight up and down, not leaning forwards towards the target or back away from it. Now put your hands on the club with your normal grip and don't worry about how strange it looks to see the club face pointing to the right (this is called an open face). Remember, this is a splash shot and the club face won't be coming into contact with the ball – all being well it'll be sliding underneath it in a flurry of sand.

Position the ball a couple of inches ahead of centre in your stance and, making sure that the club face is aiming a little to the right of your target, set up with your feet, hips and shoulders aiming a little left of the ball-to-target line. Take a full backswing and focus on hitting the sand two or three inches behind the ball. The club will slide down and underneath the ball and propel it out of the sand. The fullness of the backswing will help the club accelerate into the sand, making an explosive movement on impact. That's not the end of the shot, though: be sure to carry on with the follow-through.

Tip Remember that the sand cushions the shot and restricts the distance the ball will fly out of the bunker, so you can have a bigger swing than you would have for a shot of the same distance off the grass.

Bad lies

In a bunker a bad lie is when the ball is in a depression (such as a footprint) or is buried and is hard to get at. And when the sand is hard-packed, even if the ball is sitting cleanly on top of it, that's a bad lie. For this Maureen Madill recommends what she calls her *Australia shot*.

'This is when you use the leading – or cutting – edge of your club. Address the ball as you would for a shot off the grass, making sure that the leading edge is at right angles (square) to the ball-to-target line. Position the ball in the centre of your stance, have your hands a little in front of the ball and have your feet, hips and shoulders aiming parallel left as you would for a standard shot off the grass. This shot requires a chopping action. Its aim is to get you out of trouble effectively. Pick the club up steeply in your backswing and chop down into the sand behind the ball with some force, imagining that you're hitting all the way down to Australia.

You will have little or no follow-through because all your energies are concentrated on driving the club down into the sand and this action is what, in effect, pops the ball out. The impact will restrict your follow-through but keep going as far as you can.

All this may sound rather complicated but find yourself a practice bunker, give it a try and it should all make sense.'

figure 9.2 practise using tees at different heights above the sand

More drills

Both Nigel Blenkarne (whose many roles include being a co-founder and director of the Young Masters Golf (YMG), the Lady Masters Golf (LMG) company and group director of coaching for Crown Golf) and Derek Simpson, of The Belfry, recommend using a tee to help improve your bunker play.

Nigel says: 'This is the one shot in golf where you don't want direct contact with the ball: there should be a cushion of sand between the club face and the ball. To help get a mental picture of what you need to do, push a tee peg into the sand so that the top of the tee is about a quarter of an inch below the surface of the sand and place the ball on the tee. As you play the shot, think of striking the tee and not the ball. It works and your confidence will grow.'

Derek recommends a similar drill with a variation that sees the ball and the peg sitting above the sand. 'Tee the ball up, set up square, then open the club face slightly [remember the dial] and swing as normal, trying to hit the tee peg rather than the ball. Lower the tee peg and do the same again. Then lower it again. This gives you a great feel for the shot.'

Pitching over hazards

Of all the times on a golf course that a beginner is most likely to be at best seriously perplexed and at worst paralysed by worry and indecision it is when he or she is required to hit a ball over a hazard onto the green. The hazard will most commonly be a bunker but it can equally be a pond and whichever it is, the fear factor is liable to come into play. Usually there are no physical dangers (unless there are alligators lurking, which is not uncommon in Florida but unlikely in the UK), but if you're a beginner faced with the task of getting the ball quickly into the air, sufficiently to clear the hazard, while at the same time hitting it softly enough to stay on a green that is just the other side of the bunker or pond, the problem can appear insuperable.

The anxiety stems not only from the task of hitting the shot from behind the hazard but also from the all but certain knowledge that after you have hit the shot, you are going to be in the bunker or, worse, the pond. (The pond is worse because you're unlikely to be able to play your ball from the water and will have to drop another ball and attempt to clear the hazard again, having already lost a ball and received a one-stroke penalty.)

Many golfers, not just beginners, forget all that they've learned about how the clubs are designed to work and resort to the worst possible course of action. Anxiety takes over from common sense and reason and the player makes a tentative excuse of a backswing, then tries to scoop the ball off the ground and over the hazard. A scoop is not a shot and is virtually certain to lead to the worst possible result: your ball in the hazard.

You will see this happen time and time again – you may even be tempted to do it yourself – but don't worry, help is at hand.

Thank heavens for Evans

At Royal Porthcawl, in south Wales, the hugely respected professional Peter Evans gives extremely popular master classes to his members. He shows them how to play bunker shots and just as important, given the depth and difficulty of some of the bunkers at that great club, he teaches them how to get over bunkers.

The Evans mantra is: 'To hit the ball up, you must hit it down.'

He says: 'The pitch shot over a bunker probably presents most golfers with their severest mental challenge. Players of all categories are regularly seen tip-toeing along the fairway looking to see if their approach shot has dribbled into the bunker or whether they still have to negotiate the dreaded hazard.

Following a few simple pre-shot procedures can help you play and, most importantly, *enjoy* this demanding shot.

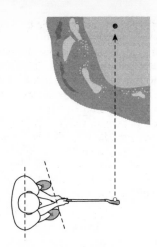

figure 9.3 an open stance

Having selected your club, usually a wedge, you must mentally rehearse the shot. Try to visualize the ball flight required. Club in hand, place its face behind the ball, making sure that it is aiming at the target and that your hands are slightly ahead of the ball.

Then take a stance with the feet, hips and shoulders aiming slightly to the left. The reason for this is that it will cause you to take the club back with a steeper backswing and consequently a steeper downswing. A steeper downswing will help to hit the ball down, to get the ball up.

Always have two or three practice swings, allowing the club to swing freely and smoothly and try to brush the ground at the bottom of the swing.'

That may sound a bit complicated but taken one step at a time, it is really quite simple. Try it in practice and you'll see how effective it is. It's worth persevering because this shot is all about confidence and the more you try it, the more likely you are to get it right. Remember the Evans mantra: 'To hit the ball up, you must hit the ball down.'

Peter's pointer

Here's a simple, very helpful Evans drill: 'I often ask players to simply stand and throw a ball with their dominant hand over the bunker to the pin. This helps simulate the ball flight required and helps create a feel for the distance.'

The last word in bunkers

Most bunkers baffle most beginners but one bunker, the Road Hole bunker on the 17th hole of the Old Course at St Andrews, terrifies almost everyone. It is not that different from a lot of the other 111 bunkers on the course because they are all fairly steep-sided and severely penal but that's not all there is to the Road Hole bunker. It faces a narrow part of the green, beyond which is the narrow metalled road that gives the hole its name and beyond that there is a wall against which people loll as they watch players struggle with one of golf's most daunting tasks. Play too strong a shot from the bunker and you will face an even more difficult recovery; play too soft a shot and you will still be in the bunker and very likely in a more difficult spot than when you started.

Through the years a great many people have suffered not just indignities but severe financial penalties for getting into this horrid little place. In fact, it is often called the Sands of Nakajima, after Tommy Nakajima, the Japanese golfer who took seven shots to escape its confines during an Open that he had a chance of winning.

In 1995 Costantino Rocca, a genial Italian, got himself into a play-off for the Open with John Daly, a free-swinging American, then got himself into the Road Hole bunker, took three to get out and that was that: Daly was the Open champion. And in 2000, David Duval, a quiet American, was lying second behind Tiger Woods on the 17th tee in the final round. Duval was in the bunker in two, took four to get out and plummeted from second place to joint 11th, an also-ran.

It's tales like this that make a round on the Old Course fraught to the end and give the Road Hole bunker its macabre lustre. The BBC have taken to burying a camera in the bunker's face, the better to record its terrors, and after the 2005 Open, with Woods again cuddling the claret jug (the Open trophy), hundreds of spectators from all over the world tramped in to take a look and take some happy snaps. They were all smiling – but only because they didn't have to play out of it.

Farewell to fear

Earlier on we talked about players being terrified of bunkers or shots that they didn't think they could play. When you think about it, it's daft, isn't it? What is there to be frightened of on the golf course? Karl Morris, the mind man, puts it all in perspective.

'It could well be that our greatest challenge at golf – or indeed life – is to overcome our inappropriate fears, being scared of things that are not actually going to harm us physically.

Fear is a tremendously useful mechanism. If I am being confronted by a pit bull terrier foaming at the mouth, then fear is probably a very good idea and a useful reaction because my body needs to be prepared to get away fast or at least be able to fend the thing off. But in so many other areas of life inappropriate fear actually keeps us stuck and limits our enjoyment of life.

I am sure that most of you will have experienced some form of fear out on the golf course, we all have. And if we have all experienced this thing called fear, the question that we need to look at is what is the actual purpose of fear? What does it do for me? What is its benefit and what effect does it have on me?

Real or imagined?

If we first of all look at the physical effects of fear, your body's reaction to fear is the same whether you are faced with a real physical threat or an imagined emotional one. Your heart rate increases, your breathing quickens, chemicals such as adrenaline flood your system preparing you for fight or flight. Not particularly useful when you're facing a soft pitch over a bunker.

You may never have thought of it this way but you have never really been frightened of a particular shot or hole at golf: what you are frightened of is the consequences of that shot or hole.

The amazing thing with many fears is that when you bring them out into the open and truly examine them, they start to fade away. Ask yourself these questions:

• What am I really afraid of?
• Is that fear useful to me?
• Am I going to let this fear stop me?

When you have asked yourself these questions, you can say *yes* to the fear that protects your life and *no* to the illusionary fears that keep us stuck in mediocrity.

When you play golf, you can now feel good about confronting your terrors and seeing them for what they are: inappropriate fears that have no place on a golf course.'

10

more hazards

In this chapter you will learn:
- to grin and bear it
- how to cope with hazards
- how to hit further.

Tip at the top

Every shot is a challenge.

Golf is a cross-country challenge and as you become more familiar with it you'll find that players, including you, tend to berate themselves terribly if they get into trouble. Now, for most of us, trouble is the order of the day in that few of us are as skilled and diligent as we might be, so our games are going to be far from perfect. Watch the professionals and you'll see that they are also far from perfect but like us (and with more reason) they expect to be perfect, so when they are not, they give themselves a hard time. Let's learn early on to be nicer to ourselves. Karl Morris gives us an insight into how to do just that.

Tune in, tune out

'So much of the time out on the course we spend inside our own head, listening in on that internal CD player of self-talk. A lot of the time what we are tuned into makes anything but pleasant listening. Yet this internal CD player will and does have a dramatic impact on how we feel and on how we play.

Think back to the last time that you played golf and just imagine if there had been a recording made of all the things that you said to yourself. If anybody else listened to this CD, do you think that they would be able to work out if you were having a good or a bad day? What would the tone be like? Encouraging, positive, upbeat? What would the dialogue be about? How capable you are, your chances of bouncing back? Where would the "voice" be coming from? Inside your head, outside, your voice or someone else's?

The amazing thing is that in most situations we would never speak to anyone else in the way that we speak to ourselves. I always tease the players by saying: "If you are going to beat yourself up, you need to do it properly!"'

Crucial

One of the key strategies for succeeding at golf and succeeding at life is to take charge of this internal CD player and start to treat yourself with a little more respect. It is one of the most important skills that you can develop for yourself, coach others and help your children to learn.

Many people absolutely torture themselves with their internal dialogue. There are many useful strategies for dealing with your CD player but for now I want you simply to become aware of what is going on at this moment. During your next couple of rounds I want you to step out of the action and just listen to what is going on. Most of this internal dialogue is so habitual and so unconscious that you are unaware of its presence and effect.

Go out next time and just tune in to what is occurring. You may even start to smile at the abuse and torture that you are inclined to inflict on yourself. After the round take a pen and jot down a couple of the things that you have said to yourself out on the course. When you actually see this on paper, you will realize how ridiculous it really is.

This first step is vital though because you can't change something unless you know what it is and realize that you're doing it.

Have fun with this and observe the self-torture your playing partners are inflicting upon themselves. Remember that there are two reactions to any shot that you ever hit: positive or neutral. Work hard at being nicer to yourself and going with the flow.'

Trees and things

Out on the course there'll be plenty of opportunities to practise your patience and make the best of things. Once a shot is done, it's done. You'll have to deal with the consequences of course but cursing yourself for something that's gone, finished, irreversible is a waste of time and you still have work to do.

One of the most famous golfing photographs ever taken was snapped at the Fulford golf course, near York, during the Benson and Hedges tournament in 1981. Phil Sheldon, who died far too early in 2005, was the photographer and the subject was Bernhard Langer, who had first climbed a tree and then folded himself into one of its forks to attempt a shot at his ball, trapped and clearly visible in another of the tree's forks.

The tree was by the 17th green and Langer, to huge applause, got the ball onto the putting surface, although sadly he neither holed the resultant putt nor went on to win the tournament. It is an apparent fact that when the total space occupied by a tree is measured it is 90 per cent air – although most golfers, and certainly Langer, would refute that.

When it comes to escapology, there has been no one better in the entire history of the game than Severiano Ballesteros. The Spaniard was a genius not just at getting out of deep rough but also in seeing ways out of a forest that no one else could visualize. He was so good that he often had to ignore the pleadings of his caddie, who would be urging him to take the safe route and chip out sideways while the Spaniard himself could see a square inch of light in the canopy of the most densely packed trees through which he was sure he could extricate his ball. Most of the time he did, too.

Walls

At the 18th hole at Crans-sur-Sierre in Switzerland, Ballesteros played what might well have been the most unbelievable single shot of his career, in a career littered with such shots. He had pushed his tee shot well to the right of the fairway and it came to rest under a profusion of pine tree branches, very close to the tall, concrete wall that protects the swimming pool. It was obvious to his caddie and anyone else watching that all he could hope to do was chip out sideways, back on to the fairway – and even that was not easy.

But the one person that the safe option was not obvious to was Ballesteros himself and soon an argument broke out between him and his caddie, Billy Foster. 'No, no, no,' Foster insisted when Ballesteros indicated his intention to blast the ball through the branches, over the wall less than six feet away, towards the green. To any onlooker the shot seemed utterly impossible but Ballesteros, knowing that he needed a birdie to have any chance of winning the tournament, was adamant it could be done. Foster knew it couldn't, but he also knew his boss, so he gave up arguing and left him to it.

Sure enough, seconds later, a great cloud of dust and dirt and grass exploded into the air, the ball soared over the wall, miraculously missed all the branches and landed on the fairway, maybe five yards short of the green. It was an astonishing shot, quite beyond not just the powers of most professionals but also totally beyond their visualization. They simply would not have 'seen' the shot.

Ballesteros, to more enormous roars, then chipped in for his birdie – but there the miracles stopped. Barry Lane, the leader, playing behind Ballesteros, hung on to win the tournament but a plaque now marks the spot where Ballesteros achieved the impossible.

Ballesteros is not a role model for the ordinary mortal. He was far too talented for that and attempting to do the things he could do will lead only to disaster. He was immensely strong, had the gift of timing and an outrageous self-belief – three things that took him to multiple major championships and three things that most of us hackers can never aspire to.

Water

Henry Longhurst, who wrote sublimely about the game and other matters and was a wonderful television commentator who used his words sparingly and wisely, once wrote: 'Splosh! One of the finest sights in the world: the other man's ball dropping in the water – preferably so that he can see it but cannot quite reach it and has therefore to leave it there, rendering himself so mad that he loses the next hole as well! Water hazards induce a degree of anger and frustration out of all proportion to their golfing consequences.'

The consequences are pretty dire though because you probably lose your ball, you may lose the hole and you certainly lose shots. Some courses are devoid of water, with not even a ditch to trouble you but elsewhere it comes in all shapes and sizes – large lakes, little lakes, puddles of ponds, streams, burns, ditches, the Pacific, the Atlantic; it can loom large or lurk unseen and it can be intimidating in the extreme. Well used by the designer it makes you think.

If you can't make the carry – that is, hit the ball far enough to clear the water, whatever its form – play around it. There's no shame in that, it's just good sense and never forget that it's not how, it's how many. Better a six or seven achieved by skirting the water than an eight or more or a blob (zero points). If you decide to play short of a stream, make sure that you really are short by taking a club that can't reach even if you hit it 100 per cent.

Seve Ballesteros (walls) – The master escapologist keeping a good grip on the situation no matter how difficult or stressful.

Also, if you're playing over a lake, say, it's not a bad thing to take a club more than you think you really need, just to be on the safe side. If you have to drive over water, pick the narrowest part and aim to carry that and if you just can't make a carry – say it's 200 yards (182 m) and your No. 1 stonker, all-time best drive is 175 yards (160 m) – play from a different tee if you can. If that's not an option, proceed to the fairway.

Some short holes, like the notorious 17th on the Stadium Course at the Tournament Players Club at Sawgrass in Florida, are completely surrounded by water (apart from a little path to get on and off the green) and you're either on (the green) or in (the water). It's only a short iron for the professionals who play it every year in The Players Championship but it's still scary. There's no way around it: no matter how good you become such holes are hard.

Rough

Rough, the long stuff that isn't closely mown like the fairway or smooth like the greens (you hope), is as varied as the courses you'll play. It may be short and fairly fine, short and thick, long and wavy, long and tough, like jungle; it may be dotted with gorse; it may be made up of heather; it may consist of whins and bracken. Whatever its composition, the rule is always the same: get the ball back onto the fairway as soon as you can. Take the shortest route back to the cut stuff and don't be greedy. Take a club that will get you out, usually a pretty lofted one like a wedge but it may be a 9-wood or a rescue club. Also known as a hybrid, a rescue club is not quite a wood and not an iron and is useful for awkward lies and extricating yourself from rough.

The only way to learn is to experiment. Find out what you can reasonably hit where and remember: no matter how strong you are, heather is tougher. Don't mess with it.

Bumpy greens

There is no getting away from it: bumpy greens are a nightmare. But if there is a consolation for beginners, it is that they are more of a nightmare for the good players than the rest. Most of the better golfers work hard to cultivate a putting stroke that will flourish on smooth surfaces and requires, more than anything, a delicacy of touch. When they are denied this, a lot of pouting usually takes place, followed by loud complaints.

What bumpy greens usually do is bring putting down to its lowest common denominator. The best technique is not your silky smooth, delicate touch but rather a good firm rap that will keep the ball on its line despite the unevenness of the surface – and everyone should be able to do that.

Bad weather

In 1979 Tom Watson won five events on the US Tour, one of which was the Memorial Tournament over Jack Nicklaus's course in Dublin, Ohio. The weather was appalling, rain combined with high winds and in one round the average score for the field was a six over par 78. That day Watson had a 72, the best score of the round and as it became obvious that he was playing so well, one observer braved the elements to go out and watch. When he got back, he was asked what he thought of Watson's play and he replied: 'Boring.' Furthermore, he meant it.

For what Watson did that day – and what anyone encountering foul weather and unable to postpone the round should do – was attend to the basics.

First of all, and most obviously, he had rainwear that both fitted snugly and kept out the weather. He had an ample supply of golf gloves because leather ones are useless when they get wet and he had several towels wrapped in a plastic bag to keep them dry. All those preparations meant that his body kept dry, his hands were dry and the grips of the clubs were dry – all prerequisites for the playing of good golf in the rain. (He also had a good caddie to help.)

Then he went out and played 'boring' golf. All he did was take one, two or even three clubs more, according to the strength of the wind, and then swing more softly, more easily. The natural effect of that was to keep the ball low and straight, meaning that in this instance he hit fairways and greens regularly, with none of that exciting stuff from out of the trees.

Anyone can do as Watson did, although whether you will win the tournament is not a given.

Two tips

Whether you are in trees, or a bunker, playing on bumpy greens or in bad weather, the word to remember is *patience*. It is pointless getting angry or frustrated, or even depressed, and just giving the ball a lash. Others will be doing that and ruining their chances.

When playing against a strong wind, the natural temptation is to try to hit the ball harder. But this is counterproductive because the ball tends to fly higher, which is not what you want. Lee Trevino always said that you should hit the ball softer because then it flies lower, so take one club more than you think you need and hit the shot more easily.

Make the rough work for you

Control, power and balance are all good things when it comes to a golf swing and Nigel Blenkarne calls this the 20-40-60-80-100 drill.

'I have used this drill extensively over the years, especially with women golfers who tend to lack clubhead speed and power. The first time was with Sarah Burnell, who went on to become an England international and a professional.

This exercise is done without a golf ball, so can easily be done anywhere there's a suitable area of semi-rough or grass that's three to four inches long. Locate your clump, take a mid-iron (a 5 or 6) and take your stance. You are going to make *five consecutive swings without pausing*.

The idea of this drill is to increase the speed of your swing *gradually*, starting with 20 per cent effort and speed, then increasing to 40 per cent, 60 per cent, 80 per cent and finally putting in 100 per cent speed and maximum effort, each time returning the club to hit the same spot of rough grass.

Make sure that each swing speed is in rhythm, making the backswing and forward swing a similar speed without stopping or pausing. It's a bit like moving through five gears in your swing. After the first 20 per cent swing is completed, swing back down and make the next backswing without hesitating at the set-up position and so on. This is continuous swinging.

This will teach you control and awareness of club speed. As a general rule you should never use your 100 per cent swing when you play but all the other speeds can be useful in shot-making and judging distance. With the help of this drill, Sarah gained 40 yards on her drives and a better sense of speed control.'

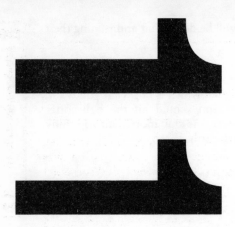

11
names you should know

In this chapter you will learn:
- about the top men
- about the top women
- about the top competitions.

Tip at the top

You don't have to be good but...

Back in the 1930s, when children did as their parents instructed, a little girl from a golfing family, whose own passion was horses, was told by her mother to keep playing golf. 'You don't have to be good,' she said, 'but when we go on holiday, you have to be able to play.'

The little girl became good enough (though never good enough to be famous) and enjoyed the game for the rest of her life but no one ever had to force the two best golfers in the world today to play and only the best that they could do was ever going to be good enough for them. If it is right that all sports should have a dominant force for the rest to look up to and aspire to, then golf is doubly fortunate in the new millennium.

Tiger Woods is the man and Annika Sorenstam is the woman and they are both leagues ahead of their competition. Neither is unbeatable, of course, for no individual or team ever is in sport but both are the person to beat in every event they enter and both prevail at a rate that has not been seen before in golf.

It has long been argued that in professional tournament golf a person who wins once a year has been successful and someone who wins twice a year has been exceedingly successful. Woods and Sorenstam have turned that adage upside down and inside out. Since becoming a professional in late 1996, Woods had, by the end of 2005, won an amazing 54 official tournaments, including no fewer than ten major championships, while Sorenstam has positively run riot among the women. From her rookie season in 1993 to the end of 2005 she won a staggering 79 tournaments, including nine majors. If Woods is dominant, then Sorenstam is overwhelming and both have raised the bar of expectation to heights never before seriously contemplated.

The greatest

For instance, Jack Nicklaus, who is still golf's most successful player with 18 major championships to his name, always used to deny, even when at his considerable peak, that he entertained any thoughts of completing the Grand Slam – the winning of the four major championships in a calendar year. The first of these is the (US) Masters, which is held in April every year at the Augusta National Golf Club in Augusta, Georgia. This is followed in June by the US Open Championship, in July by the British Open (more properly called just the Open) and in August by the US PGA Championship. These events represent the four peaks in the men's game and it is by winning these that a golfer's career is measured. A player can win any amount of money in any number of regular tour events but unless he wins at least one major championship he is never going to be given the accolade of being a 'great' golfer.

Nicklaus, indubitably great, admitted that to raise your game to the heights needed to win a major in four specified weeks of the year was just too difficult: the combination required of good form and good luck coming along at the right time was too unlikely. In his case he was right. Although he won two of the four in the same year on no fewer than five occasions, he never won three and the Slam was always beyond him.

Compare and contrast the position taken by Woods, whose attitude is that while the Slam is indeed improbable, it is certainly possible and, as an admitted perfectionist, it is in his thoughts at the start of every season. His quest starts at Augusta, where the immaculately prepared course with its undulating, lightning fast greens suits his game and by the end of 2005 he had won the tournament four times. But in 1997, when he won the Green Jacket (presented to the Masters champion) for the first time, he was 19th, 24th and 29th in his next three majors; in 2001 he was 12th, 25th and 29th; and in 2002, although he won the US Open for a second consecutive major, he was 28th and second in the next two.

Perhaps Woods's best chance disappeared in 2005 when, after winning the Masters, he appeared certain to win the US Open as well, until he made a series of late mistakes and Michael Campbell, of New Zealand, produced some superb play to take the trophy. Woods went on to win the Open at St Andrews and who knows what he might have done had he gone to Baltusrol, in New Jersey, for the US PGA, as holder of the first three championships? As it was, he shared fourth place and so a season in which he finished first, second, first and fourth was dubbed by some as a failure!

Tiger Slam

The original Grand Slam, achieved by the great Bobby Jones, an amateur, in 1930, consisted of the amateur championships of the US and Britain and the Open Championships of both countries and will never be emulated, but if the modern calendar Slam has eluded Woods, it has to be said that the greatest achievement in golf so far belongs to him. In 2000 he won the US Open, the Open, the US PGA and then, in 2001, the US Masters. He held all four of the major championships at the same time, and many people were prepared to call that a Grand Slam. But Woods himself never quite did. 'I've got all four at the same time,' he would say. 'All four trophies are on my mantlepiece and no one else can say that.' Tellingly, although Colin Montgomerie was one of many professionals prepared to call it the Grand Slam, Tiger's father, Earl, never did, and it remains one of his son's ambitions.

Very good

Montgomerie has yet to win a major but after the 2005 season, he had won the European Tour's Order of Merit, the Premiership title if you will, eight times, double the previous best (by Peter Oosterhuis and Seve Ballesteros) including an unprecedented seven in succession. The Scot was undoubtedly good enough to win a major during that period but the fact that he did not, losing, unluckily, twice in play-offs, counts against him when assessing the great players.

The elite

Nicklaus's record of 18 professional majors, seven ahead of Walter Hagen, a flamboyant character whose heyday was in the Roaring 1920s, is what Woods has his eye on. He is now ahead of Ben Hogan, a legendary American and Gary Player, a battling South African. Tom Watson, an American who won the Open five times, has eight, with Arnold Palmer, a swashbuckling American icon credited with being the catalyst for the golf boom in the 1960s (Arnie's Army was the name given to his legions of fans) in the list on seven.

Colin Montgomerie – A major force in European golf, the Scot's swing is all his own but it's rhythmic, it repeats and it suits him.

Alongside him are Sam Snead and three players from another era entirely: Harry Vardon, Gene Sarazen and Bobby Jones, the gentleman amateur from Atlanta who co-founded the tournament that became the Masters in 1934 and was revered by all who knew him and millions who didn't. Nick Faldo, the best British golfer of the modern era, has six and Ballesteros, the most extravagantly talented European to play the game, has five. Modern giants like Vijay Singh, of Fiji and Ernie Els, of South Africa, have three. Two more of today's big names have two each: the quiet, sweet-swinging South African Retief Goosen and the big-hitting left-hander from California, Phil Mickelson. John Daly, an American whose erratic game is the epitome of steadiness compared to the soap opera that his life has been, has also won two – the PGA Championship of 1991 and the Open of 1995. Winning two majors is quite a feat but winning more than that starts to separate a man from the rest. It is the ultimate measure of a player.

The eye of the tiger

Not only did Nicklaus set the benchmark for all who follow with his 18 major championships, he also had no fewer than 19 runner-up places. He won his first major, the US Open, aged 22 and he won his last, the US Masters, aged 46 and for large parts of that time he was the dominant force in the world game. Beat Nicklaus and win was everyone else's slogan. He was, and is, the target at which Woods aims. On the young Woods's bedroom wall there was a chart listing all the great man's achievements – now there is a Woods versus Nicklaus section on Tiger's website – and it has been his everlasting ambition to surpass them, such is the mark that Nicklaus has left on the game.

Dubbed the Golden Bear, Nicklaus was probably the longest hitter the sport has ever known. Today's players, with their modern clubs and balls developed with new technology, hit the ball a little further than Nicklaus did but whereas he was 50 or 60 yards (46 or 55 m) ahead of his contemporaries, Woods and Els, today's big hitters, are no more than 10 or 20 yards (9 or 18 m) ahead of theirs. Watching him when he was in his late twenties and early thirties was to be awed by his strength and technique. To stand close to him when he was straining for that extra yard was to be almost frightened that something would burst – a knee, an elbow, a vein in his forehead – or maybe just the club face or shaft.

Nicklaus was not just a big hitter. He had the coolest, most analytical mind on a golf course and was able to make good decisions under the most intense pressure. And in the final analysis he holed more pressure putts than anyone ever has, although Woods has so far equalled him in that department.

The swashbuckler

The undercard, as the boxing men have it, has been marvellous for many years. Severiano Ballesteros, for instance, the dashing Spaniard, the handsome hitter, the maker of marvellous, magical recoveries and the man all other men longed to be. He was the embodiment of that piratical figure who, sword between his teeth, rescues the maiden from the evil-doers who have dragged her off. He won his first championship, the Masters, aged 22 and at that point it seemed likely that he would be able to translate an outrageous talent into at least one major a year and so threaten Nicklaus's 18. But although Seve was to dominate the European scene, to become the golfer that everyone had to beat and rarely did, to be the attraction for every sponsor, he never fully realized his potential. He finished with just five majors, two Masters and three Opens, which was a poor return for someone so good.

Part of the reason was the fact that he was dragging the European Tour upwards and onwards and, as the major figure, felt he had a right to appearance money. Despite the Tour outlawing such a thing, ways around it were not difficult to find. But that brought problems too because Seve, an exceedingly proud and stubborn man, felt it his duty to give value for money and so he tried his utmost, even in the pre-tournament pro-am. One of his caddies said, memorably, that he had never before worked with a player who, if he needed six birdies on the last six holes to win or even to make the cut, fully believed that he would achieve those six birdies. Absolutely and completely believed it. So Seve tried and tried and tried, even when he should have been more relaxed and eventually he burned himself out. There were physical problems along the way – a bad back plagued his career – but Seve should have been in double figures in major wins.

The grinder

Nick Faldo was the complete opposite of Ballesteros. Never a great ball striker, he made the absolute most of his talent, working as hard as any golfer who ever lived to ensure that nothing that could be learned was missed out. He famously took two years to remodel his swing under the tutelage of David Leadbetter because he felt the swing with which he had already been successful would not stand up to the pressure of the final round of a major championship. After doing that, Faldo went on to win three Opens and three Masters, to become the second most successful British golfer in history. Vardon, in the early years of the last century, won six Opens and one US Open.

Faldo could be a dour, uncommunicative man, likely to refuse to talk to anyone if the round he had just completed did not please him for any reason. He had constant battles with the media, both on and off the course but he was BBC Sports Personality of the Year in 1989 (after the first of his Open wins) and he has also been made an MBE. These days he is more amenable, still competing but spending more time commentating insightfully on television and designing exceedingly good golf courses.

There was never any doubting Faldo's abilities, particularly in the Ryder Cup, the biennial match between Europe and the United States, where he was Europe's great deliverer of points. Perhaps his finest hour came at Oak Hill, in Rochester, New York, in the 1995 match when Europe desperately needed him to beat Curtis Strange in the final singles series. Faldo was one down with two to play but won the 17th and was all square on the 18th tee. He then drove into the rough and had to play short not just of the green but of a steep bank of tangled grass in front of it. He was left with a 93-yard shot which, with incredible precision, he wedged to four feet. Strange missed his par putt, Faldo, nerves jangling, holed and Europe had conjured an amazing victory.

Cup competitions

In addition to the four majors, there are five well-established Cups, all of which are played every two years on a home and away basis. They are the Ryder Cup, between the male professionals of the US and Europe (first contested in 1927 and donated by Samuel Ryder, a seed merchant from St Albans); the Solheim Cup, between their female counterparts (named after Karsten Solheim, the inventive genius behind the Ping company, and his wife Louise); the Walker Cup, between the male amateurs of the US and of Great Britain and Ireland (taking its name from George Herbert Walker, who was president of the United States Golf Association in 1920); the Curtis Cup, between their female counterparts (presented by the sisters

Harriot and Margaret Curtis, who won the US Women's Amateur four times between them); and lastly the relative newcomer, the Presidents Cup, between the male professionals of the USA and those of the rest of the world, barring Europe, known as the International team.

Blood and guts

There is something about international team match play that generates huge drama and Gary Player, who has twice captained the International team in the Presidents Cup, called it the 'raw blood and guts' of the game. All these Cups can be, and frequently are, incredibly exciting, especially as levels of ability throughout the world are rising to the extent that the dominance of the Americans, once a given, has been demolished in recent times. There is rarely more than a point or two in any of the results, although in the last Ryder Cup, played at Oakland Hills, near Detroit, in 2004, the home team were defeated by the amazing margin of 18½ points to 9½. This was a result brought about by the fact that the Europeans fielded what was probably the strongest team in their history.

The Ryder Cup is now played at 12-a-side and, back in 1987, when the matches were at Muirfield Village in Ohio (Jack Nicklaus's course, designed and nurtured by him) Europe managed to win with a team that contained six reasonable players in Gordon Brand Jnr, Ken Brown, Howard Clark, Eamonn Darcy, Jose Rivero and Sam Torrance and six outstanding ones, five of whom were major champions: Nick Faldo, Ian Woosnam, Severiano Ballesteros, Sandy Lyle and Bernhard Langer, plus Jose Maria Olazabal who would become one. Darcy, an Irishman with a unique swing, holed the winning putt but it was a desperately close call.

Team spirit

By 2004 there was not a single major champion in Europe's team but the overall level of ability was enormously improved and in cricket terms the team batted all the way down the order. Furthermore, they appeared to embrace each other as a team, whereas the Americans, all multi-millionaires, many of them with their own jets, appeared either not to know or to care about the team concept. They denied that but the impression remained and was reinforced by the attitude of one member of the team, Chris Riley.

After playing just one match on the first day, he was paired with Tiger Woods on the morning of the second, and won, handsomely by 4 and 3, against Darren Clarke and Ian Poulter. But when Hal Sutton, the American captain, proposed playing Riley and Woods together again in the afternoon, the former declared that he was too tired and would rather rest. Too tired, at the age of 30, after two 18-hole matches in two days? Too tired to play with Tiger Woods? Too tired to exhaust yourself playing for your country? Woods, who had appeared to enjoy himself playing with Riley, played instead with Davis Love III – and lost. It was differences of attitude of that kind that helped Europe to their stunning victory.

It is probable, though, that the nine-point margin in 2004 will be a one-off – there is simply not that amount of difference in ability between the two teams and once the Americans immerse themselves in a 'one for all and all for one' attitude they will surely come roaring back.

Formidable

Oddly enough, the last time there was anything like that number of points between the teams was in 1981, when the Ryder Cup was played at Walton Heath in Surrey – and the score was exactly reversed, with Europe getting the 9 1/2. The American team that year was probably the strongest golf team ever fielded for any match in the history of the sport. For the record, it consisted of Jack Nicklaus, Tom Watson, Lee Trevino, Johnny Miller, Raymond Floyd, Hale Irwin, Jerry Pate, Ben Crenshaw, Larry Nelson, Bill Rogers and Tom Kite. Oh, and Bruce Lietzke, a hugely talented player who was the only one of the 12 who was not, or did not become, a major champion.

Europe's response was to appoint Tony Jacklin as captain and he helped change the Ryder Cup for ever. The combative Jacklin had been a major influence on British golf ever since he won the Open in 1969, the first home-grown golfer to do so since Max Faulkner in 1951. For a brief spell Jacklin was unstoppable and inside 12 months went on to win the US Open. Both wins were well deserved and it seemed at that point that Britain had acquired a world beater. But Jacklin never won another major. His next realistic chance came in the 1972 Open at Muirfield but not only did he not win, he was also destroyed as a championship golfer. He was to say years later: 'I was never the same man after that.'

Despair

Jacklin and Lee Trevino were fighting out the final stages and on the long 17th it seemed as if Jacklin had prevailed. Trevino was in trouble from the start and as they walked together towards the green, the talkative American said: 'It's all yours, Tony.' Jacklin was just short of the green in two, Trevino had seen his fourth shot race through the green and into some deep and straggly grass on a steep bank at the back of the green. From there he seemed certain to take at least three more, for a double bogey seven, while Jacklin, with a simple chip, might well make a birdie four or at worst a five and have a lead of two or three strokes with one to play.

Trevino took a casual swipe at his ball and, against all the odds, it ran and ran – into the hole. Jacklin, who had chipped to about 15 feet, was aghast at what was for him a blatant stroke of ill fortune and he promptly lost his concentration. His first putt ran about three feet past the hole and in a horrified silence he missed the one back. He had taken six to Trevino's incredibly lucky five and had, on that green, lost the Open Championship. He never got over it.

The inspiration

That aside, Jacklin's influence on European golf continued when, in 1983, he took over the captaincy of the Ryder Cup team. He was an inspirational captain, a man who knew his players and how to get them to play their best and he transformed the Ryder Cup scene. He insisted on the best of everything – clothing, flights, facilities – and in 1983, in Florida, Europe lost by a single point and it was Ballesteros (later an inspirational captain himself at Valderrama) who recognized the significance of the result. As the players were sitting in the locker room, dejected at having lost by such a narrow margin, it was the Spaniard who jumped to his feet and said: 'Why are you all so sad? This was a great victory. And next time we will [expletive deleted] them.'

Jacklin captained Europe in the next three matches, winning the first two and halving the third before standing down. His success was helped by the fact that Europe by that time had developed some fine players, with Ballesteros, Faldo, Lyle, Woosnam and Langer, who were all born within 12 months of each other, providing the backbone of the team.

Sandy Lyle – A wonderful striker of the ball, the Shropshire-born Scot won an Open and a Masters.

Wonderful women

The Solheim Cup is another contest that has brought wonderful excitement. It began in 1990 at Lake Nona, in Orlando, Florida, amidst trepidation on the European side, whose history in women's professional golf was almost non-existent compared to that of the Americans. The women's tour in Europe was barely out of its infancy and anyone good enough to have ambitions had to try and join, and survive on, the women's tour in America. That first match was lost comfortably but, to the astonishment of everyone, the next match, at Dalmahoy, in Edinburgh, was won by Europe.

Upset

The home team were fuelled by some comments made by one of the American players, who said that only one, possibly two, of the European team stood a chance, on ability, of getting into the American team. It may have been close to the truth but it was the sort of thing that should have remained an unspoken thought and by coming out with it to an American magazine she only stoked the fires of the Europeans, who played their best golf. Captained by Mickey Walker, Helen Alfredsson, Laura Davies, Florence Descampe, Kitrina Douglas, Trish Johnson, Liselotte Neumann, Alison Nicholas, Catrin Nilsmark, Dale Reid and Pam Wright won by $11^1/_2$ to $6^1/_2$, a result which remains one of the great sporting upsets.

The US were to win the next three matches, with a points differential of 46 to 30, before Europe managed to win at Loch Lomond in 2000. The picturesque Scottish course is situated in one of the five wettest places in the British Isles and it was only because of the importance of the occasion that the match was played in waterlogged conditions. Europe seemed to have brought the superior water wings, winning by $14^1/_2$ to $11^1/_2$ on what quickly became known as the boggy, boggy banks of Loch Lomond.

Sweden

Europe won again in 2003 when the match went to Sweden for the first time in recognition of the tremendous contribution Swedish players had made to European golf, with the likes of the incomparable Sorenstam, Neumann, Alfredsson, Sophie Gustafson, Carin Koch, Nilsmark and Pia Nilsson, an inspirational coach, leading the way over the years. Nilsmark, crippled by a bad back, was captain and led a team of three Swedes, three Scots, one Spaniard, one Norwegian, one Dane, one German, one Frenchwoman and one Englishwoman to victory by 17 points to 11. The margin owed something to total confusion at the end when, with the match decided, there were still five individual games on the course. Instead of playing to a finish, as is traditional, there were concessions all round and the true extent of the triumph will never be properly known. What was not in doubt was the overall success of the contest. It was superbly organized by the Swedes at the lovely Barseback course, not far from Malmo. Some 150,000 spectators attended during the week and the atmosphere, especially for those of a European persuasion, was electric.

The 2005 match, at Crooked Stick in Indiana, was lost by the Europeans after a promising start, but the early fears, back in the 1990s, that America would always be too strong, have not materialized and a scoreline, after nine editions, of 6–3 to the United States, is encouraging. And the match is going back to Sweden in 2007!

The amateurs

The Walker Cup was for many years a virtual non-starter as far as victories for Great Britain and Ireland were concerned. Begun officially in 1922, the series has been dominated statistically by the Americans, to the tune of winning 32 of the 40 matches, with one halved. That figure, though, is slightly misleading in terms of the relative strengths of men's amateur golf in the US and Great Britain and Ireland as it applies in the last ten years. Throughout the 1920s and 1930s the US did not lose a match and lost precious few thereafter – 1971 at St Andrews was one memorable exception – until we get to the year 1995 and a glorious win for Great Britain and Ireland on a glorious golf course, Royal Porthcawl. That was the occasion when Tiger Woods came to the last hole level with Gary Wolstenholme, whom he outdrove by as much as 60 yards (55 m) throughout. After their tee shots at the 18th, Wolstenholme had to hit a 5-wood into the green, Woods had only a 9-iron. Remarkably the Englishman found the green, Woods found out of bounds, and lost.

Although the match in 1987 was won by America, Great Britain and Ireland, heavily influenced by Peter McEvoy, variously captain and chief selector, won the next three on the trot although the USA reversed their losing trend with a narrow one-point victory at Chicago Golf Club in 2005.

As in professional golf, there is a levelling up of talent, with players from many countries taking advantage of the US college system, which offers scholarships to talented individuals but in McEvoy, Great Britain and Ireland possessed an exceptional leader, who knew how to get the best from his players.

Curtis

The Curtis Cup is the female counterpart to the Walker Cup and like the men, the British and Irish women had a dismal record in the earliest days of the matches, which began in 1932 at Wentworth. The Americans immediately started a winnng streak that has led to the overall series (prior to 2006) standing at 24 wins for the US, six for Great Britain and Ireland, with three halved. Again, though, like the men, the record is far, far better in more modern times, there being a period between 1986 and 1996 when, of the six matches played, Great Britain and Ireland won four and halved one.

Prairie Dunes

The win in 1986, at Prairie Dunes, a sublime course in Kansas, was positively historic. It was the first time an international golf team, male or female, amateur or professional, had gone to America and won. Europe's pros managed to replicate the feat the following year in the Ryder Cup and the Walker Cup was won in Atlanta in 1989 – but the women got there first. Nor was it a fluke. The margin of 13–5 to the visitors reflected not just the superiority of the players but of their attitude.

In the match of 1984, the Americans had prevailed by just one point and Diane Bailey, the home captain, came to believe that Great Britain and Ireland had golfers just as good as the Americans, they just had to be made to realize it. She worked hard to instil confidence in her team for the next match and it worked beautifully – especially when mixed with a little indignation thanks to the comments by one of the American players. It was Danielle Ammaccapane who, on the first day on the first tee, casually remarked to her captain: 'We always win this thing, don't we?' and roused the visitors to play their best.

Women to watch

It's well worth watching the good amateurs because so many of them go on to the top of their profession and it's a joy to watch them progress. The women, even with Sorenstam in such stellar form, tend to get overlooked but for most of us less gifted golfers they're the ones to watch because they do not generate the awesome power of the men and have to rely more on rhythm and timing, just the things that we need to concentrate on. They also tend to be more accessible.

Sorenstam's dream

Sorenstam does not share the superstition that lofty aims should be kept to yourself. The Swede declared at the start of 2004 that her target was the Grand Slam and when she didn't achieve it, missing out in the first major of the season, she said that it would be her aim to do it in 2005. She got the golf world very excited when she won the first two majors, the Kraft Nabisco and the McDonald's LPGA championships. There was a huge turnout of press and television at the Cherry Hills Golf Club in Denver, Colorado, for the third championship of the year, the US Women's Open, which Sorenstam had already won twice – but she barely figured in the event and was equal twenty-third.

It is a championship in which the woman who is arguably the best of all time, has a mixed history. After she won the event in 1995 and 1996 it looked as though she might win it every year thereafter, such was her ascendancy. Indeed, her sponsors Callaway, the club manufacturers, prepared a series of advertisements to boast about her third successive win. No one has ever won the championship three years in succession and in her attempt to do so – to three-peat as the Americans say – Sorenstam missed the cut. The ads were never shown.

The fact that she came nowhere near winning the US Women's Open in 2005 and was barely in contention in the final championship, the Weetabix Women's British Open, at Royal Birkdale just serves to illustrate the difficulty of achieving a Slam but Sorenstam will keep trying.

Stunning

The Weetabix is the latest addition to the women's championship schedule, coming in as a replacement for the duMaurier event in Canada, which was a victim of a ban on tobacco advertising.

Annika Sorenstam (Sorenslam) – The Worlds No.1 woman golfer applies ferocious concentration and determination to every shot.

The event is already acquiring a rich history, one that includes the best start to a final round ever made in championship golf. It was achieved by the Kent golfer Karen Stupples at Sunningdale in 2004. The first two holes, for the women, are par fives and Stupples played the first in three, for an eagle, and then holed her second shot at the second, for an albatross. That made her five under par for the first two holes, gave her the lead and she went on to win her first major.

The future

If Sorenstam is currently miles ahead of her opposition, the next few years will be fascinating as Michelle Wie, Paula Creamer and Morgan Pressel seek to catch up. The three American teenagers are outstanding talents, with Wie, the youngest, having become the most talked about female golfer in the world. This was because she was still in her early teens, tall and graceful in fashion-model style and able to play golf to a standard matched by few. She also enjoys playing against the men on the US Tour when invited, and although she had yet to make a cut by the end of 2005, the publicity generated by the very fact of her playing has led to vastly increased publicity for any tournament concerned and an extremely high profile for her.

Wie turned professional in October 2005, on her sixteenth birthday with 'signing on' fees from Nike and Sony totalling US$10 million, the most hyped female golfer of all time. Now all she has to do is justify it.

In the pink

Creamer has already gone some way to doing that. Only 19 in 2005, the confident teenager won twice in her rookie season on the LPGA Tour (and twice on visits to Japan) and is already considered one of the players to beat. With good looks accompanied by a ready smile, she is going to make a fortune off the course and, with her ability on it there for all to see, another fortune with her golf clubs. Pressel, the US Women's Amateur champion, has also turned professional and is expecting great things of herself. There is also Ai Miyazato, of Japan, to watch. Already adored at home, she is ready to take the rest of the world by storm and at the end of 2005 gave due warning that she is a player of some substance by winning the LPGA qualifying school by no fewer than 12 shots. Sorenstam is her idol and inspiration.

Laura Davies – Britain's finest woman golfer. No holding back; the peripatetic Englishwoman has won all over the world.

The grande dame

There is no way that Laura Davies, now in her forties, can be overlooked. The tall, big-hitting blonde Englishwoman has been the one constant in terms of a British presence in the upper echelons of the women's game and with four majors to her name and dozens of tournaments and millions of dollars won on the women's tours around the world, she has had a charismatic career with which she is well satisfied. There have been few golfers more gifted and in addition to her individual achievements – she won the US Women's Open in 1987, paving the way for Neumann (1988), Sorenstam and Alison Nicholas (1997) – she has had immense moments in the Solheim Cup. At Dalmahoy she was unstoppable and unbeaten and an American official, seeking to express just how good she had been, said: 'If Laura played like that every week on tour she would win ten million dollars a year.' Davies, who had been drained by the intensity of her efforts and whose aversion to practice was infamous, smiled and said: 'Oh no I wouldn't. I'd be in the loony bin.'

12

joys ahead

In this chapter you will learn:
- the treats that are in store
- the names of some great courses
- you'll never play them all.

Tip at the top

There is no such thing as a bad golf course.

It's a great tip and a philosophy espoused by Pat Ruddy, an eclectic Irishman of golf, who has built some lovely courses himself. He's right but you'll develop your own personal preferences and naturally some courses are better than others, as you'll come to appreciate. But British and Irish beginners are more blessed than anyone from any other part of the world. They have more to look forward to, in the way of superb courses, when they become competent golfers, than any of their counterparts elsewhere – and all of them are on the doorstep. Americans, for instance, have to travel huge distances and pay out vast sums to experience the unparalleled delights of links golf that are so readily available in England, Scotland, Ireland and Wales.

Scotland claims the title of 'Home of Golf', while Ireland probably has more high-class courses to the density of population than anywhere else. England has some gems and Wales, having captured the staging of the Ryder Cup for the year 2010, has set about letting everyone into the secret by promoting the superb courses it has to offer.

Almost all of the courses in the four countries mentioned are open to visitors. Some clubs, like Muirfield in Scotland and Royal St George's in England, can be a little aloof and are harder to crack but they are far from impossible, whatever you may hear. They will often respond to a nicely written letter assuring them that you have a handicap and are not going to dig up their precious course (or arrive in jeans).

There are two aspects of golf that are unique and a huge attraction to all who play it. First of all anyone with a semi-decent game can play on any of the world's great stages. If Scotland is the home of golf, then St Andrews is where the home fires are kept burning. The Old Course is frequently voted the best course in the world and hosts the Open Championship regularly, yet it is a public course on which, with a bit of organization and determination, anyone can play.

Veritable hackers can, and do, play the Old Course at St Andrews, a unique situation in sport, insofar as a parks footballer could not play competitively at Wembley or a club tennis player at Wimbledon. The other aspect is that thanks to the handicapping system anyone with a handicap can play anybody else, up to and including (in theory anyway) Tiger Woods, and hope to beat them.

Most of the courses here will ask that you have a handicap and a certificate from your club or society or driving range pro to verify it. Having got one, you have the key to an unsurpassable store of golfing riches. It would be next to impossible, even in a lifetime, to play all the wonderful courses in Britain and Ireland, of which the following are only a tiny proportion. They are nearly all links courses, too, because it is the presence of so many of this type of golf course that separates these islands from the rest of the world. To be a true links the course must be built on land which 'links' the arable pastures further inland and the coast. The defining characteristic is that it will probably have been covered by the sea at some stage in its life and will have a sandy subsoil covered by fine fescue grasses. This will usually mean that in summer at least the fairways will be dry, hard and fast, the greens harder and faster and while your drives will go further because they roll more, the shot to the green becomes extremely hard to stop anywhere near the pin. Links courses are where the game originated and it is they that present its truest test.

The ultimate

St Andrews

The ultimate links course is the Old Course at St Andrews, where the Open Championship is played every few years. But just as links courses are themselves completely different from parkland or heathland courses, so St Andrews is unique among links courses. Not only does it start and finish in the middle of town, it also has seven enormous double greens, each serving as a putting surface for two holes. They start at the 2nd, which shares a green with the 16th and they go on from there, the 3rd sharing with the 15th and so on until finally the 8th shares with the 10th. The trick to remembering them is to know that when the hole numbers are added together, the total always comes to 18.

St Andrews was designed by no known architect: it just came into being and although regarded by many as a museum piece, it still challenges the best golfers in the world. The ball now goes much further than it used to but even with technology threatening to overtake the game, it has still been the really good players in world golf that have triumphed on the Old Course. The winner of the Open in 2005 and 2000 was Tiger Woods, unquestionably the finest player in the world since Jack Nicklaus; the winner in 1995 was John Daly; and in 1990, Nick Faldo. As the winners in the years before that were Seve Ballesteros (1984) and Nicklaus (1978), it can be seen that it takes someone special to win there.

It would take more space than there is in this whole book to talk in any detail about all the great courses in Scotland but here, in alphabetical order, are some that simply should not be missed: Carnoustie, Dunbar, Gullane, Kingsbarns, Muirfield, Nairn, North Berwick, Royal Dornoch, Royal Troon and Turnberry.

Not for the faint-hearted

Carnoustie

Carnoustie is not a course to be tackled lightly. It has the justified reputation of being one of the hardest golf courses in the world, with hole after hole testing players to their limits – and in many cases beyond them. Furthermore, just when the player, having survived thus far, thinks that at least it can't get any harder, it does.

The 16th is allegedly a short hole but at 230-odd yards, into the prevailing wind, it can often be a full driver shot off the tee, even for the good players. The 17th is a long par four, requiring two almost perfect shots to reach the green and the 18th, a par five for most of the time, becomes a par four when the professionals come to town. The big worry is the Barry Burn that crosses the fairway in front of the green and when the wind is off the North sea, it is almost uncarryable. This was the hazard that Jean Van de Velde infamously got himself into in the 1999 Open and, needing a six to win, took seven – then lost in a play-off. The uniqueness of golf is that you too can attempt that fiendishly difficult finish, you too can try to carry the Barry Burn – and there is every possibility that you could take the five that Van de Velde would have sold his soul for.

A fair test

Muirfield

Muirfield is the favourite championship course of many golfers, largely because it is held to be the fairest test of them all. There is only one really 'blind' shot where you cannot see the green or the pin, the rest is laid out before you and what a test it is. In the 1989 Open, Nick Faldo, in dreadful weather, played each hole in exact par, won the championship and was labelled 'boring' for the manner of the victory. That was nonsense because on that course in those conditions each par was a triumph and it is hugely to the credit of the Englishman that he was able to bear down and, ultimately, win.

Royal Dornoch

Royal Dornoch is a long way from almost everywhere – when you get to Inverness, you think you are nearly there but there are still 50-odd miles (80 km) to go – but it is definitely worth what is almost like a pilgrimage. It is a wonderful links and the world's top golfers, like Tom Watson, winner of eight major championships, have made it their business to go and play there and departed delighted.

Just up the road from Dornoch is the tiny town of Golspie, with a lovely quirky golf course designed by James Braid, one of the Great Triumvirate, with Harry Vardon and J. H. Taylor, who dominated the Open Championship in the early years of the twentieth century. Just down the road is Tain, designed by an even earlier great, Old Tom Morris, who won the Open four times between the years 1861 and 1867 and it is one of the glories of golf that places like Golspie and Tain lie there waiting to be discovered.

Further south

When the Open Championship comes to England, it is hosted by Royal St George's, Royal Birkdale, Royal Lytham and St Annes and in 2006, for the first time since 1967, Royal Liverpool, or Hoylake as it is more familiarly known. They are all wonderful courses and although George's, in Sandwich, Kent, is an intensely private club, it will yield to polite persistence and the others are much less restrictive. Birkdale,

Lytham and Hoylake, in the north-west, are part of what the tourist people have dubbed England's golf coast and it is one of the greatest strips of golfing territory in the United Kingdom and a dream destination for a golf holiday. Look into the possibilities of going to Hillside, next door to Birkdale, to Formby, and to Southport and Ainsdale just down the road. They are all great places to play and you'll discover other gems like Formby Ladies', Heswall, Hesketh, Wallasey and West Lancashire, to name just a few.

Birkdale

Birkdale has entertained every great golf event worthy of the name and yet it need not be an overpowering experience. There are tees for all levels of ability, although if the wind blows everyone can be in trouble. The course was the scene of one of the great moments of all time in golf when, in the 1969 Ryder Cup, Jack Nicklaus and Tony Jacklin played each other in the last match of the contest, one that would decide the destination of the Cup. They came to the last all square and if the match stayed that way, the entire contest would end as a tie. Eventually Jacklin had a two-and-a-half foot putt to halve the hole and Nicklaus stepped forward, picked up Jacklin's ball and said: 'Tony, I don't think you would have missed that putt, but I didn't want to give you that chance.' The conceded putt meant that the Cup ended as a halved match and both sides held the trophy for a year. Nowadays we're meaner and the holder retains, with no sharing.

It is said that some of Nicklaus's teammates were furious with him for not making Jacklin hole out but Nicklaus was always a supreme sportsman. He came second in major championships no fewer than 19 times and never failed to look his opponent in the eye, shake his hand and congratulate him sincerely.

Royal St George's

Royal St George's is another course to have hosted all the great tournaments, the most recent of which, in 2003, brought about one of the great golfing shocks. Ben Curtis, a complete unknown at the time, won the Open. He was ranked 396th in the world when he arrived in England, he was playing his first major championship anywhere and was quoted as a 750–1 shot by the bookies. He needed lots of luck to win, and it came when Thomas Bjorn, the great Dane, who was three shots ahead with four holes to play, dropped a shot at the 15th and then hit his tee shot at the short 16th into a bunker. Instead of making sure he got out first time, Bjorn tried to be a bit too clever and saw his ball roll back into the sand. Then he tried the same shot again, with the same result. The third time he got it out and holed the putt for a double bogey five – but his lead had gone. After another dropped shot at the 17th so were his chances and Curtis became the unlikeliest Open champion of all time.

Deal

There is plenty of wonderful golf to be had in the vicinity of George's. Royal Cinque Ports, more commonly known as Deal, is a classic British links and in many ways preferable to its more famous neighbour. The clubhouse is friendlier, the club itself more welcoming and the course itself both fairer and more manageable – good reasons all for going there. On the other side, with some holes bordering the 14th of George's, is Prince's, where they actively court your custom. It's where Gene Sarazen won the Open in 1932.

There are many other outstanding courses in England, not least the wonderful cluster in Surrey that includes Sunningdale, Worplesdon, St George's Hill, Wentworth and Walton Heath. The Berkshire is a favourite and further afield and simply not to be missed are St Enodoc in Cornwall, Silloth in Cumbria, Ganton in Yorkshire and Woodhall Spa in Lincolnshire. Keep practising and start saving.

Cymru

Wales has always had some great golf courses, it's just that it has never boasted about them. That is changing now as the Welsh realize just what they have been missing in terms of golf tourism. Having snaffled the 2010 Ryder Cup from under the noses of the Scots, they have mounted a big publicity drive to promote courses that are as good as anything to be found in the UK.

Royal Porthcawl

Royal Porthcawl, in South Wales, is the outstanding course in the country and has hosted a Curtis Cup, a Walker Cup and the Amateur Championship on several occasions. With a few changes it would be quite good enough to host an Open Championship, too, although the club itself seems not to want to go down that route. It is one of the few links courses where you can see the sea from every hole – and occasionally you can feel it as well on the first three holes. All three border the beach and when the wind really gets up from its prevailing quarter, the south-west, it whips sea spray and sand all down the golfer's left side. At least it sometimes helps to blow a shot hit left back onto the course.

As is so often the case in Britain and Ireland, there are other wonderful courses close by and a golf holiday in the area is an enticing prospect. Pyle and Kenfig is just up the road, Southerndown and Ashburnham are no distance at all, while Pennard, on the lovely Gower Peninsula, is an absolute gem that very few know about.

Royal St David's and Aberdyfi

In the middle of Wales there is Royal St David's, one of the most scenic courses anywhere, with Harlech Castle glowering over the links and Aberdyfi which is a joy. Aberdyfi was the absolute favourite of Bernard Darwin, the first golf writer, who wrote for *The Times* and was good enough to play for Great Britain and Ireland in the Walker Cup. Darwin played his first golf on family holidays at Aberdovey (Anglicized version) and remembered winning a club tournament with a score of precisely 100, which, considering his eventual eminence, gives hope to us all.

Ireland

In 2005, the IRA finally put down its guns and called a permanent ceasefire and that means that some of the greatest courses in the world can now be put back on everyone's schedule, for there are probably more must-play courses in Ireland, pro rata, than anywhere else in the world. So much so that it is difficult to know where to start and space demands that there can only be a passing mention for many of them.

A totally arbitrary top six would comprise, going in an anticlockwise direction around the island from Dublin: Portmarnock, Baltray, Royal County Down, Royal Portrush, Ballybunion and The European Club at Brittas Bay. Any of these courses could host any of the world's top tournaments and three of them are ranked in the American magazine *Golf Digest's* 100 best courses outside the United States. They are Portrush (3), County Down (4) and Ballybunion (7). Portmarnock is ranked 30, The European Club, designed by Ruddy, vastly underrated, is 61 and – in a way thankfully – Baltray, also called County Louth, does not make the list at all. I say thankfully because it may remain a secret gem for a little while longer.

Portrush once hosted the Open in 1951, the only time the championship has been held off the British mainland and it was won by the ebullient Englishman Max Faulkner – but not before he had tempted all the fates, and survived. Faulkner, leading after three rounds, was asked to autograph a ball and did so, signing himself 'Max Faulkner, Open champion, 1951'. No shrinking violet he, he then made it come to pass in the fourth and final round.

Portrush boasts some magnificent holes, while Royal County Down boasts some magnificent scenery, as well as testing holes. In fact County Down is arguably the most photogenic golf course in the world, with the mountains of Mourne sweeping down to the sea and it is a great pleasure to play.

Some Americans argue that Ballybunion is the greatest links in the world and it is difficult to argue with them. Certainly some of the seaside holes are spectacular, the scenery such that it is tempting to just sit down and look at it and give up on the golf for a while. On Ireland's wild west coast, it is too far from civilization for major championships to be held there and the small eponymous town does not have anything like the required amount of accommodation. But the course is certainly of the right calibre and no visit to Ireland would be complete without playing there.

The European club is another delight in store, a course where the owners will get you on if they possibly can. 'The object of the exercise,' says Ruddy, the owner of the club, 'is to have the clubhouse open at about 8 a.m. and the kettle on.' As you may have guessed, the hospitality is superb and, when you get to it, so is the golf course. Built by Ruddy himself, it is the epitome of links golf and well worth a ranking in the top ten, never mind coming in at 61. That's the great thing about rankings, though, you can spend a lifetime devising your own.

It would take years to play all the courses on the Irish coastline, as wherever you go there seems to be a must-play just around the corner and it takes no great golfing detective to discover them. But, as the briefest of guidelines, here are a few suggestions to start with, heading north from Dublin and sticking to the coast: The Island, Portstewart, Castlerock, Ballyliffin, Portsalon, Rosapenna, Rosses Point, Enniscrone, Belmullet, Lahinch, Tralee, Ceann Sibeal and Waterville. And that barely scratches the Irish surface.

In fact, far from being extensive, the list of the courses of all four countries is basic at best. Did we mention Boat of Garten, Little Aston, Rye, Conwy, Dooks, Connemara? There are literally hundreds more and the great delight of the game is that you can go and discover them for yourselves. And then, of course, there's the continent of Europe and beyond.

A step back

One of the joys of golf is its infinite variety. Not only is every golf course totally different from every other one, even the same golf course never plays the same way twice, as wind and weather in general do their work. Anyone who has been a member at a club for any length of time knows that a hole which is, on one day, a drive and 6-iron, will be, on another day, a 3-wood and 9-iron – or anything in between.

These variations, enjoyable and essential as they are, are part of the game's appeal. It's a constant, if ever-changing challenge and if you really want a test of what the game is like, there's more. For the last few years it has been possible, in a quiet corner of West Virginia, to play the game as it was in the late 1800s, on what is acknowledged to be the oldest golf course in America.

Oakhurst Links

It is called Oakhurst Links – and this is a course with a real difference. For a start, you are not allowed to use your own clubs, your own golf balls, not even your own tees. All your equipment must be hired at the course itself, for golf at Oakhurst is played with hickory-shafted golf clubs, with gutta percha golf balls and from tees made with a pile of earth or sand – just as it was when the course came into existence in 1884.

Oakhurst is but a baffy (an ancient name for a lofted driver) shot or two away from The Greenbrier, a huge luxury resort that has hosted both the Ryder Cup and the Solheim Cup. Its venerable neighbour is owned by Louis Keller, a scratch golfer in his day and a playing companion of the great Ben Hogan and

Sam Snead. Having bought the property principally for its stabling, Keller, encouraged by Snead and other enthusiasts, rediscovered the golf course and lovingly restored it as an astounding, living museum piece.

It is thought that the course came into being largely because of the building of a nearby railway linking Washington DC and Charleston, West Virginia. A large number of Scots were employed on this project and naturally they wanted somewhere to play their game. The landowner at the time, Russell Montague, agreed to set aside some of it for a golf course and when it opened, with just six members, it was the first in the United States. It thrived at first but when the railroad was completed many of the members moved away and by 1910 Oakhurst was in decline.

The use of the word astounding to describe today's Oakhurst is not just hype. Having to use the modern reproductions of that ancient equipment really does bring home to a golfer of any standard just how astoundingly far the game has moved on in the last 120 years or so. The golf clubs, being comparatively light and whippy, require to be swung in a totally different manner in order to get any kind of firm hit and the ball, to modern hands, feels like a stone. Gutta percha comes from the Malaysian tree *Palaquium gutta* and its sap, when boiled, becomes malleable.

In the early days they shaped balls by hand, although moulds were later introduced so that the result was at least more uniformly round. Unsatisfactory though they now seem to be, it was not until the early 1900s that they were superseded by a ball made of wound rubber, the Haskell as it was called, after its inventor.

But to get back to Oakhurst. A visit there will enable you, for a very reasonable fee, to hire five hickories and two gutties and play the 9-hole lay out twice. You get instructions, too, including the rule that if your gutty breaks in two, as they sometimes do, then the hole must be completed with the larger part.

It is not, at first sight, a long course and you may look askance at a hole of some 390 yards (356 m) proclaiming itself to be a par five. But by the time you get there you will realize that unless you are a very good golfer indeed and have, furthermore, adapted to the strangeness of the equipment completely, then you simply will not be able to reach the green in two shots. (Snead, with his sweet swing and hustler's heart, was happy to take on all-comers.)

It is a salutary experience and one that increases our knowledge of what went before and our admiration for the old-timers who won championships with such implements. It is another of the deep-seated pleasures to be had out of the playing of golf.

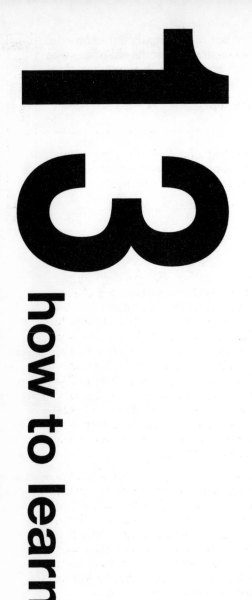

13
how to learn

In this chapter you will learn:
- a practice routine
- the benefits of good coaching
- to listen judiciously.

Tip at the top

Golfers who know learn from a pro.

Can you really learn golf by reading a book? Is it really possible to reproduce all the seemingly complicated series of movements in a golf swing by absorbing it from the printed page?

The answer is yes, and here is a true tale that proves it.

Toogood

Anyone who has played golf to a reasonable standard knows that the most difficult thing in the world is to completely change a swing that has been at least moderately successful. In recent years Nick Faldo attempted to do just that but he had the help of a dedicated coach in David Leadbetter and all the video and swing aids that exist in these modern times. Ditto Tiger Woods with Hank Haney. But back in 1948 there was no such thing as video or television and in the backwoods that was Tasmania at that time, there were hardly any golf books even. There was, though, one very promising golfer who, at the age of 18, had won both the Tasmanian amateur and Open championships and went on to become one of the outstanding amateurs in the period since the end of the Second World War.

His name was Peter Toogood, son of Alf, the professional at Kingston Beach and the young man thought he had a pretty good swing until one day his father said: 'I think you need to become more consistent. I'd like you to swing more like Byron Nelson.' At that time Nelson was to golf what Tiger Woods is today. In fact, he was even more dominant. In 1945 Nelson won 11 tournaments in succession and while two of them were matchplay, he averaged 67.8 for the remaining nine strokeplay events. No wonder Alf wanted his son to swing like him.

Model sequence

But how to do it? Without television, without DVDs, without the internet? Peter Toogood tells the story: 'My father got hold of a book by Nelson and tore out a swing sequence. He pasted those photographs on either side of our fireplace at home and so every evening we had nothing to look at but the Byron Nelson swing! I have to admit making those changes was agonizing but dad insisted that it would work if I kept at it. It took about 18 months but I then had a solid, robust style for the remainder of my years in competitive golf.'

The authors can vouch for that. Playing with him at Royal Hobart, his home club, when he was 71, it was clear that his swing had stood the test of advancing years so well that he could beat his age anytime that he felt like it. And we haven't been the only people impressed by the simple elegance of the Toogood swing.

When the inaugural World Amateur Team Championship was held at St Andrews in 1958, Toogood was part of the four-man Australian team that eventually won the event. He had the lowest score in the tournament in the third round and to his astonishment was summoned to the hotel room where the captain of the American team was staying.

As that captain was Bobby Jones, the greatest amateur of all time and the winner of 13 major championships (second only to the 18 of Jack Nicklaus), Toogood was mystified as to what he could want and was a little worried. It turned out that Jones, who was by then crippled but had followed the match from a specially adapted buggy, wanted to congratulate the Australian. 'He commented on my long and straight tee shots,' Toogood recalled, 'and then asked me how I had developed the American type swing in faraway Tasmania when only a few players outside America had by then adopted it.

A look of disbelief crossed his face when I told him of my boyhood swing change struggles and the Byron Nelson photographs hung on the family fireplace by my father.'

More than by the book

So it can be done, but the best thing about living in the here and now is that reading this book need not be the only source of golfing wisdom. Combine it with visits first of all to a PGA qualified professional and then to a driving range or practice area. Peter Toogood had the advantage of expert guidance from his father, who was an accomplished teacher and competitor and long and hard as the young man studied those photos, he did not absorb their message by osmosis alone. He went to the practice ground and made what he had seen come to life in his own swing. His reward, a lifetime of good golf, can be yours too.

Toogood, who remained an amateur, became a physical education teacher and was a huge influence on golf in his native state. He was also involved in setting up the Australasian Golf Museum at Bothwell in Tasmania, the site of the first golf course in Australia. In the foreword to *Simply Toogood*, an absorbing biography by Des Tobin, Norman Von Nida, a legendary Australian professional, wrote of Peter: 'Because of his skill and trust in his own ability, together with his mental approach to golf and his attitude to life, I have no doubt whatsoever that he could have had a highly successful professional career. He has also made a remarkable contribution to education, junior golf and golf administration in Tasmania. He has taught, coached, mentored and has passed on his love of and respect for the game of golf to countless young Tasmanians. These young people have been fortunate indeed, for they could not have had a better mentor or role model to guide them than Peter.'

This, then, is a man who had made a close study of the game and has a deep understanding of it. He is well worth listening to and here are some of his thoughts.

'Golfers of all ages – particularly club golfers – who want to improve their game need to understand that consistency, improvement and confidence come as a result of correct basic skills and technique, organized practice, sound concentration and sensible course management. For any golfer who seriously wants to learn the basic skills on which to build an individual style and method of play it is essential to have lessons, preferably from a local golf professional.

There is no one particular method of swinging a golf club that works best for everyone. It is basically made up of simple, logical movements, the essential elements of which are the grip, the address or set-up, head position throughout the swing, release, follow-through and most of all balance. Any golfer not playing well should check these basics...a regular or periodic lesson with a club professional is strongly recommended.

Pace your practice

The club member may have limited opportunities for practice but "good" practice for 20–30 minutes is more likely to improve technique and scoring than two to three hours on the practice range aimlessly hitting balls with no real purpose. Good practice develops confidence in your own method and involves setting goals or targets to achieve within a given practice period. Avoid tiredness. If arm muscles become fatigued take a break. Practising when fatigued can cause bad habits to develop and can lead to loss of concentration and confidence.

Golfers should develop an individual, consistent method of hitting a ball. If you are to develop consistency and scoring improvement, it is essential that certain fundamentals are developed and built on during good practice sessions. These fundamentals include the correct grip, head position at impact, consistent rhythm, weight transference and body balance in the hitting position and at the finish of each shot, whether it be a drive, fairway metal shot, long or short iron, chip, bunker shot or putt.

Good purposeful practice improves skill, technique and concentration and this is a routine that any golfer can follow.

1 For the first four to five shots of your practice session, relax and "feel" the rhythm in your swing. Know where your head and hands are throughout the swing. Feel the rhythm in your feet and legs. You can use any club to achieve this but a 9-iron or 8-iron is best for this exercise. Do not be concerned with the result of the shot. Remember, this is all about feel.

2 As you hit the next ten to 15 shots try to imagine the perfect swing and flight of the ball as you hit each shot. This is called imagery.

3 For the next ten to 15 minutes set targets such as trying to "lob" the ball on a certain spot or area. Try hitting five to ten consecutive shots between two flags or two trees in the distance. Restart from step one when a shot is not successful. Include plenty of variety in this practice exercise. This helps develop better concentration.

4 Regardless of where the ball goes, practise certain aspects of your swing that the club professional may have suggested to improve your swing. This is called the mechanics of the swing and it may help to have another person observe and comment.

5 Complete your practice period by swinging quietly searching for that feeling, rhythm and timing by hitting shots a certain distance regardless of the club used. You may even find the ball will travel further than expected.

Instinct

Bobby Jones believed that practising deliberately to *feel* the action of hitting a ball a required distance is an important skill that should be learned, practised and then employed when playing a round of golf. The thing I remember most about my conversation with him was his unswerving belief that golfers should on most occasions go with their own instincts when facing a particular type of shot. I have never forgotten that advice and have passed it on to hundreds of junior golfers that have passed through my programmes over many years.'

Diversity

The amazing and wonderful thing about golf is that there is no single style, no one way to play it. Bob Torrance, the legendary Scot who is father of former Ryder Cup captain Sam and one of the world's great coaches, says: 'There are certain basic principles which can and should be taught to everyone – but each individual will still have a unique swing.

A simple visit to the practice driving range at any tournament will emphasize the truth of that. In recent times two of the most successful golfers that Britain has produced have been Lee Westwood and Darren Clarke and, as they are good friends, they often practise together. But there is absolutely no similarity in the outline of their swings. They both go about the essential business of presenting the club face square to the ball at the moment of impact in totally different ways. Neither of them is wrong, for the golf swing is bound to look different when the club is swung by all the various shapes and sizes that we human beings come in.

Torrance himself likes to suggest that a comparison be made between Ben Hogan and Jack Nicklaus, two of the greatest golfers the world has ever known. Hogan, with his distinctive style, was forever fighting a hook; Nicklaus played all his best golf with a fade. As Torrance says: 'Those two dominated the game in their eras, yet their swings were poles apart.'

1 Address position

2 Takeaway

3 Thumbs up

4 Top of the backswing

5 Starting down

figure 13.1 a good swing sequence with a short iron

6 Approaching impact

7 The moment of truth

8 Into the follow through

9 And on ...

10 To ...

11 A balanced finished

He might have included Lee Trevino, whose swing, among the great players, was unique and yet took him to six major championships, or Sandy Lyle, winner of the Open and the Masters, who had a swing that only he could reproduce with any consistency.

All these champions had at least one thing in common and it is replicated by all the great players that have ever existed. To go back to Torrance: 'To become good at this game there is no alternative to investing in long hours of practice.'

The right coach

Having said that, it is not the slightest bit of use practising the wrong thing. You will get some idea of the basic principles involved in playing golf from this book but to flesh them out it is important not just to find a coach but to find one that you get on with, one that you understand – and who understands you. Coaches are, like golfers, different, with different ways of explaining the same thing and it is not always the first coach you find that will be the best for you. Make sure that you both know what you want, for instance. One distinguished Scotsman, a teacher of note, was driven to despair by a large lady who had lessons every day for a month but made no progress. 'I gie up lassie,' he said. 'It's nae use because you'll never make a gowfer in this world.' She replied, with stunning clarity, 'I don't want to be a golfer. I never ever said I did. I am only taking lessons to reduce.'

One of the great, great coaches of our time, now semi-retired, is John Jacobs, who was instrumental in the early progress of Jose Maria Olazabal, the Spanish Ryder Cup player and twice US Masters champion. Once, when the Spaniard was in a slump, Jacobs was asked to look at his swing and said afterwards: 'I only needed to see him hit three balls before I knew what was wrong. But it took me two hours to find the right words to get through to him what he needed to do.'

After that lesson Olazabal came second in the tournament in which he was competing that week – his highest finish for two years – and two months later he won the Masters.

Jacobs once took just 15 minutes to sort out Jack Nicklaus, who was preparing for the Open Championship at Royal Lytham in 1969. At the 1st and 3rd holes Nicklaus hit huge slices onto, or possibly even over, the railway line bordering the course and he hit another huge slice at the 6th, 50 yards right of where he wanted to be. At that point Nicklaus called to Jacobs, 'Whaddya think, John? You're supposed to know these things.'

Jacobs recalls: 'Jack's posture was so bad that the back of his neck was almost parallel to the ground.' He was stooped so far over the ball that he couldn't make a proper turn and once Jacobs had pointed this out, Nicklaus recognized an old fault and said, 'Jack Grout often says he wants to give me a right hook, just to get me standing to the ball correctly.'

Grout

Nicklaus admits that he was lucky that Grout, his first coach was exactly the right man for him. In his autobiography, *My Story*, he says: 'If Jack had not arrived at my father's club at the same time that I began to take up the game, aged ten, right now I would probably be selling insurance from Monday to Friday and going fishing for my weekend fun.'

Famously, even when winning major championships on a regular basis, Nicklaus would go back to Grout at the start of every season for an 'overhaul'. He would ask the coach to check the essentials like grip, stance and posture – and frequently found that in the stress of the previous season something had slipped and needed correction. 'Just when a fellow thinks he's finally got it,' says Nicklaus, 'along comes another problem and there he is scrambling for the secret again.'

There is no such thing as 'the secret' of course but no one wants to admit that and it seems that the better the player the more reluctant he or she is to acknowledge that immutable fact. What else could explain Tiger Woods, after winning all that the game could offer including eight major championships between 1997 and 2002, changing his coach Butch Harmon and moving to another in Hank Haney?

Woods spent two years playing at a lot less than his best, winning no majors but all the time insisting that he would come back eventually a better player than ever before. Well, the jury is still out on that one. Woods has started to win majors again but not at the rate that he did before – it was a fast pace that he set – and with a swing that many feel has made him demonstrably more erratic than he was before.

Woods is not the only player to seek perfection, of course, and back in the 1980s Nicklaus did much the same thing, albeit changing his game with the same coach. He admitted: 'I don't know what Tiger was doing but I do know he's much like I was from the standpoint that I never relied on what I had as being what I wanted. I always wanted to get better. I had a terrible year in 1979 so I went back to Jack Grout and said: "I need to do some things that will make me a better player."' This was a man who had already won 15 major championships and so, presumably, had been doing something right. But he wasn't satisfied, and he and Grout revamped his swing, he spent three months working on the changes and then, in April 1980, won the Masters. By that time, though, Nicklaus was 40 and fighting the inevitable decline that comes to all sportsmen. He won only two more majors.

The PGA

The right coach, then, is an important asset on the road towards a successful golf game. To take the first steps the easiest thing to do is to consult the website of the Professional Golfers' Association (PGA) which will not only give a list of its professionals at the clubs near to your postcode but will also, through the RAC, provide a route map to get you to your chosen club.

You could also try the *Yellow Pages*, which will have a list of golf clubs and driving ranges in your area and the *Golfer's Handbook* is an invaluable tome, full of fascinating information and a comprehensive list of the clubs and courses in the British Isles and Europe. It lists addresses, telephone numbers, websites, location, green fees and more, including the name of the pro, if there is one.

The PGA is an amazing body, having celebrated its centenary in 2001 with a membership of more than 7,000, working on every continent around the globe. Broadly speaking its job is to look after its members throughout the world to ensure the highest standards of coaching and, in modern parlance, to grow the game.

This means encouraging development at every level, from junior to adult, girls and boys, men and women, from established players to the estimated 2.4 million casual golfers in England alone who are not actually members of a club. To this end PGA professionals provide, at certain times of the year, periods of free coaching. Their counterparts in the United States do this too and in 2005, during what they call Free Lesson Month, the PGA of America set a new record, with an astonishing 122,160 lessons given by 6,889 professionals throughout the country.

In its early years the PGA was the only body in the UK charged with looking after the country's professionals and it was to the PGA that Samuel Ryder presented the Ryder Cup. Ryder was a highly successful seed merchant, having hit on the idea of selling his seeds in little packets – and made a packet from so doing. He was a late entrant into the game of golf but became besotted by the game and eventually gave the superb trophy for the contest that bears his name, the Ryder Cup. This has become one of the world's greatest sporting events, although the European Tour, which looks after the tournament professionals, is now much more involved in matters. The PGA still owns the actual trophy and works together with the Tour, which now, as far as the Ryder Cup matches are concerned, calls itself the Managing Partner, while the PGA is the Founding Partner.

Beginnings

The founding fathers of the PGA were three players who, in the older and more grandiose days of journalism, became known as the Great Triumvirate. It was an apt, if overblown, description of Harry Vardon, James Braid and J. H. (John Henry) Taylor, a trio who between them won 17 major championships in the 20 years from 1894. Vardon, in fact, is still the most successful English golfer in terms of majors, having won the Open on six occasions and the US Open once, in 1900, when J. H. was runner-up. Vardon's seven majors place him one above Nick Faldo, a fact not generally appreciated.

It was Vardon after whom the most popular grip in golf, the Vardon grip, was named, and while the great man did not claim to have invented this particular way of holding the club, it was his adoption of it that made it popular.

The R&A

The Royal and Ancient may sound aloof and fuddy-duddyish but does a great job in regulating the game and in organizing tournaments such as the Open Championship.

It takes its name from the Royal and Ancient Golf Club of St Andrews, which came into existence in 1754 and in 1897 became the governing authority on the rules of golf. The club's members are all male – there are no plans to have any female members – and generally white and middle-aged but they have always had the best interests of the game at heart. They, and their opposite numbers in the United States Golf Association (USGA) (who have once had a woman as president), make a big point of the fact that they only rule 'by consent' of the people they make the rules for.

In 2004, for legal and practical reasons, there was a complete re-structuring of how things work. The R&A is still golf's most important ruling body but the rules bit has been transferred to a body called R&A Rules Limited – there is also R&A Championships Limited, R&A Group Services Limited and The R&A Foundation, all of which has confused some of the members no end. R&A Rules Limited is responsible for the rules and governance of golf all around the world, except for the USA and Mexico, where the writ of the USGA runs.

Wide-ranging responsibility

You can get some idea of the extent of the R&A's involvement with the game when you realize its scope. 'We operate with the consent of more than 125 national and international, amateur and professional organizations, from over 110 countries and on behalf of an estimated 28 million golfers in Europe, Africa, Asia-Pacific and the Americas outside the USA and Mexico.'

The R&A has an awesome responsibility, for not only does it have to decide on and promulgate the rules, it also has to ensure that the spirit of the game remains intact – something that is under challenge from the incredible strides in new technology. For a whole host of reasons – space-age materials in club and ball manufacture, better-conditioned courses, bigger and stronger players – the ball is now travelling incredible distances. This is a source of great fun and satisfaction to many but the problem is that it is rendering a great many golf courses if not obsolete then certainly less challenging. It will eventually be up to the R&A and the USGA in concert to decide whether or not to 'freeze' the game, whether to say so far and no further or to let technology have its head.

It is not an enviable position to be in. If those twin authorities decide, for instance, that the distance the ball goes must be limited, the ball manufacturers' first reaction will probably be: 'See you in court', claiming that they are being subjected to an unfair restraint of trade. Similarly, if they decide that the clubs are too powerful, those manufacturers will cry foul. But if the authorities simply do nothing, then clubs around the world will have to spend tens of millions of pounds lengthening their courses to cope with the effects of the new technology. Talk about being between a rock and a hard place.

Munificence

The R&A chief executive is Peter Dawson, a county standard golfer in his youth and subsequently a successful businessman before being recruited to St Andrews. In a relatively short time he has revolutionized the way the R&A goes about its business, while at the same time maximizing the profits made by the Open Championship.

The latter is important, not because any money goes either to the club or to the members of the R&A but because the club is able to distribute largesse around the globe. In the years 2004 to 2010 it plans to give away the enormous sum of at least £50 million – all of it from operating profits from the Open.

The R&A is responsible for running a great many events through the year and hugely successful they are too. The Open is arguably the world championship of golf, its field comprising a much larger element of golfers from all over the world than any of the other three major championships. Thanks to its incredible popularity, and some consequently huge television rights fees (191 territories worldwide were reached in 2004), the Open makes a big profit, large amounts of which go on the promotion of every aspect of the game in every corner where it is played.

For instance, some of that money recently provided a triple mower to cut the greens at the Uganda Golf Club as it prepared to host the All-African Team Championship and, closer to home, 11 universities were provided with funding for their golf programmes. Altogether, countries as diverse as Russia, China, Italy, Namibia, Bulgaria, Puerto Rico and Argentina have been visited by Duncan Weir, the R&A's director of golf development.

Great though that is, the R&A could do more if golf were to be accepted as an Olympic sport. Within the game there are mixed beliefs as to whether this would be a good thing and whether the sport needs any addition to its present format with its concentration on the four major championships. But the other aspect of the argument is that if golf became an Olympic sport then throughout the world the game would become eligible for the same kind of government grants that go already to established Olympic disciplines. As some of the more backward, in golfing terms, countries in Europe and elsewhere desperately need more funding, the more the R&A can do to ensure they get it, the better.

The application for golf to be included in the 2012 London Games was turned down and Dawson said: 'There can be no doubt that Olympic golf would have given a tremendous boost to the development of the game in emerging golf nations around the world. But we have to accept that we must now find other ways to fund the game in these countries and also that golf will remain outside the Olympic movement for the foreseeable future.'

Close links

Clearly there are areas where the PGA and the R&A can help each other and in 2005, at a meeting at the PGA's headquarters at The Belfry in Sutton Coldfield, ties were strengthened and close co-operation agreed upon. *R&A News* reported that 'where aid is considered appropriate, a golf professional is recommended by the PGA of Europe to become that country's golf development consultant. The consultant meets relevant officials, visits any existing golf courses, talks to those who currently provide any golf programmes, meets the country's most promising players, conducts golf clinics and explores the possibility of state support.' It is a pretty comprehensive programme and one that should see golf booming in places where it now has a mere toehold.

Vacancies

One of the great things about coming into the game nowadays is that most golf clubs throughout the United Kingdom are looking for members. For a long time many of those same clubs had waiting lists for membership and it could sometimes take five years or more before a vacancy opened up and an applicant was accepted. That was always a short-sighted policy, in that the longer the wait the less likely it was that the applicant would still want to join when he or she was eventually invited. In recent times there has been a fall in membership numbers across the board and in a survey carried out by the English Golf Union (EGU) and the English Ladies' Golf Association (ELGA) in 2004 they found that the average number of vacancies in golf clubs in England was 51.

So most clubs will have room for more members but there are likely to be some restrictions. For instance, many of them will not be keen on accepting a total beginner: they would far prefer that he or she has reached the stage where they can at least propel the ball forwards a reasonable distance and also that they have an adequate knowledge of the rules and the way the game is played.

The cost

Another restriction is purely practical – the twin financial problems of the entrance and membership fees. At first sight these seem to be hefty, with the average membership fee for a male at an English club being in the region of £560 and for a female £510. Add to that the average entrance or joining fee of £670 for men and £615 for women and it can be seen that in the first year the male applicant will have to stump up, on average, £1,230 and his female counterpart £1,125. That can come hard but thereafter golf club membership is incredibly good value. Take the average annual fee of £560 and simply divide it by the weeks in the year and you will find that you are paying just a little less than £11 a week for unlimited rounds of golf. It is an unpopular thought but it is quite possible that golf club membership is too cheap rather than too expensive, given the cost of maintaining the clubhouse and the course in good condition!

Joining a club

Given, then, that you have decided that you would like to join a club nearby, how do you go about it? That EGU/ELGA survey shows that a simple written application to the club secretary is the most common method (18 per cent), followed by being proposed by a current member (14 per cent). There will usually be an interview at some stage of the proceedings but whereas once this ranked with taking the boy/girlfriend home to mother on the stress scale, it is now likely to be far more informal.

Some beginners can be shy about ringing a club because there is a popular misconception that they are exclusive places, for the elite only. This could still be true in perhaps one per cent of clubs but certainly not in the other 99 per cent. They will be glad to hear from you, if for no other reason than you are likely to be a source of revenue for the club and the resident professional.

Hanging on to new converts to the game is frequently the difficult bit but of those who were new to the game when they took part in Free Lesson Month, 83 per cent continued to play golf, averaging an encouraging 17 rounds in the next 12 months. It was estimated that in doing that they spent US$1,661, or about £960 on their game – so you are valuable, a real asset.

It is not necessary, of course, to join a private club to play golf. Almost every club in the country operates on a pay-and-play policy, allowing visitors to play for the payment of a one-off green fee. It may be that at some of them you have to arrange to play in advance, mostly in order to avoid clashing with the visit of a society, or perhaps a club competition, and it may also be more difficult at weekends. But a few phone calls are usually all it needs to find a time and place to play.

Munis

There are also more than 100 municipal courses dotted around the country in seven regions, where again a one-off green fee is paid. These tend to be more accessible but occasionally less well-kept, than their private club cousins – and they are also extremely popular.

In Birmingham, for instance, one course, Pype Hayes, was in such demand that in order to get a game on a Saturday, would-be golfers started queuing late on Friday night, sleeping in their cars outside the gate to the club so as to be among the first on the course. The act of queuing itself became an institution at one time, to the point where the golfers were bringing sandwiches and flasks of coffee for breakfast and, in one extreme case, a portable gas stove for the bacon and eggs! Nowadays, though, the municipal clubs in Birmingham have installed a pre-booking system which, while it may be much more efficient, is not quite so romantic.

Concluding thought

Gillian Burrell is one of the most respected teachers in Ireland, who dispenses her wisdom at the Stepaside Driving Range in Dublin. She believes in setting the scene for learning before burdening you with too much technical information but we're all inclined to listen to siren voices and she cautions all beginners: 'Don't confuse yourself by taking technical advice except from a qualified PGA professional. Almost everyone who plays golf (and even some who don't) is a so-called expert and even though they are only trying to help they usually end up hindering your progress. They're the sort of people who counsel: "1 Keep your head down; 2 Keep your head still; 3 Keep your left arm straight." I call these miss concepts: they're more miss than hit and they tend to be bandied about willy-nilly, leading to confusion and lack of improvement. Let's take them one by one.

1 If the golfer buries his head on his chest, it will invariably lift as he comes down to impact. This "head down" syndrome also causes poor posture and limits your shoulder turning underneath your chin. Most golfers use "keep your head down" as a panacea for everything that goes wrong with a golf shot. Usually you have simply topped the shot (failed to get the ball airborne). Just concentrate on hitting the bottom of the ball.

2 If you keep your head completely still, you will limit your ability to transfer your weight over your back leg, which in most sports is the principle of dynamic motion. Try throwing an object as far as you can keeping your head still. Now try throwing the same object but let your head move naturally as you try to generate power. Notice which one goes further. It is okay for your head to move laterally by about two inches (five centimetres) before any real damage is done. (But if you are flexible enough to keep your head still without difficulty, all the better.)

3 If the left arm is kept rigid throughout the swing, the arms will work independently of the body and prevent the turning of the left shoulder. It will also make the swing rigid and may also contribute to injury. Better that both arms are gently pressed towards each other at address. This relaxed starting position will certainly lead to better motion.

Head south

A player can have good fundamentals and a sound swing but if the clubhead makes contact with the wrong part of the ball it will not get airborne. Look at the golf ball as a globe and notice the difference in your ball flight when you hit the North Pole, the Equator or the South Pole. See which one flies the best and practise until you repeatedly find the South Pole. Don't give up. This skill is acquired over a period of time with plenty of practice.

Remember, it's the game for a lifetime. Enjoy.'

ace A hole-in-one, a 40,000 to 1 chance for the average player, or approximately one every 1,000 rounds played.

address The position taken up prior to hitting the ball.

air shot To miss the ball completely (when trying to hit it).

albatross Like the bird, a real rarity. It's a score of three under par and realistically can only be achieved by holing a second shot at a par five, although there have been instances of players holing in one at a par four.

all square When level with your opponent in a match.

approach shot A shot with a short iron to the green.

away The ball furthest away from the pin.

back nine Holes 10–18, the second or home nine, the inward half.

back marker Player with lowest handicap in the group.

back tee The tee furthest away from the hole, used for competitions.

backspin When the ball comes back towards the player on landing.

backswing The first part of the swing as the club moves away from the ball to the top of the swing.

bag drop Area, usually in front of the clubhouse, where you can leave your clubs when you arrive to play; more common in America than in Britain and Ireland.

ball marker Used to mark the position of the ball on the putting green, a small coin or flat disc.

better ball match A match in which two players form a team to take on another two, with only one score to count from each team.

birdie One below par, thought to originate from the American slang of the early 1900s when the term 'a bird of a shot' meant one that finished successfully.

bisque A shot given in a friendly match that the recipient can choose to take at any time.

blading An action that sends the ball skittering along the ground, usually unintentional.

blaster Another name for a sand iron.

blind shot A shot where the desired target cannot be seen.

bogey One over par, for example taking five at a par four; a double bogey would be a six; a triple bogey a seven; and so on.

borrow/break The contours to be assessed when looking to hole a putt or play a chip or pitch shot.

buggy Common name for a motorized golf cart, prevalent (often compulsory) in America, where it is more common to ride around the golf course than to walk; they make the clubs a lot of money but defeat the exercise object of the game.

bunker An obstacle made difficult by being filled with sand.

caddie (or caddy) Person who carries a player's clubs, offers advice on the course and how to play it.

call through To invite the group behind to play through your group if they are having to wait, usually done when searching for a ball.

card Official score card of the course.

carry The distance a ball 'carries' through the air.

chip Also 'chip and run', a short, low shot played around the green so that it runs towards the hole.

choke Slang term for losing your nerve, to collapse under pressure.

choke down To hold the club further down the grip.

committee In golf the committee running the tournament sets the rules for the competition.

concede A term of surrender – to give a putt, or a hole or a match.

cut A cut shot veers to the right (if you're right-handed); also a term used in professional events when a cut in the number of competitors is made on the basis of the best 70 or so scores; usually made after 36 holes of a 72-hole event; hence 'to make the cut' means to survive for the last two rounds; if a pro misses the cut, he or she makes no money (as a general rule).

dead A ball so close to the hole that the putt cannot be missed.

divot Turf removed in the course of playing a shot.

dog-leg A hole shaped like a dog's hind leg, bending either right or left.

dormie The situation in match play when a player is as many holes up as there are left to play and so cannot be beaten; not applicable if extra holes are to be played.

draw shot A shot intentionally made to move from right to left (by a right-hander).

driver A club designed with minimum loft to give tee shots maximum distance.

driving accuracy Statistics have become commonplace on the professional tours of the world and can be useful in working out what areas of the game need attention; driving accuracy on the European Tour is defined as the number of fairways hit from the tee.

driving distance The Tour measures two drives, on holes chosen to counteract the effect of gradient and wind and the distance travelled, regardless of whether the shot finishes on the fairway or not, is then averaged.

duck hook Slang for a shot that flies low and very sharply left (if hit by a right-hander).

duff To hit behind the ball and barely move it at all.

eagle Score that is two under par on one hole, for example a three at a par five.

Eisenhower Trophy Men's World Amateur Team Championship, held every two years.

Espirito Santo Women's World Amateur Team Championship, held every two years.

etiquette A fancy word for good manners on the golf course.

explosion shot Recovery shot from a bunker.

fade Opposite of draw, a ball that is intentionally moved from left to right (by a right-hander).

fairway Mown grass between the tee and the green.

flag/flagstick Marks the position of the hole on the green; also called the pin.

flier A ball that goes further than it should because when hit from rough, the grass nullifies the spin, unjudgeable and dreaded by the pros.

flop shot An advanced shot played so that the ball rises almost vertically into the air and 'flops' down onto the green.

fluff A bad mis-hit.

fore Shouted loudly when there is a danger that the players in front may be hit; comes from 'Before'.

follow-through The part of the swing after hitting the ball.

fourball Four players hit their own ball; a fourball match pits two against two, the best score of the respective partnerships to count (as in better ball).

foursomes Two players in partnership hit alternate shots with one ball.

fringe The area of short cut grass that is just a little longer than the putting surface, which it surrounds.

front nine Holes 1–9, the first nine or outward half.

gimme *See dead.*

greenkeeper/greens staff Literally 'the keeper of the green' which, in golf, is the entire course, not just the putting surface.

greens in regulation Arguably the most important statistic of all, a player records a GIR when reaching the putting surface in the recommended number of shots or less on any given hole; one for par threes, two for par fours and three for par fives.

ground under repair (GUR) Area of course officially marked as unfit for play, entitling the player to move the ball away, without penalty.

hacker The politest term, of many derogatory ones, for a player whose skills leave something to be desired; players may also use it self-deprecatingly of themselves.

half A hole is halved when completed in the same number of shots as the opponent(s); a match is halved when players are tied or level on the last green.

handicap A system of allocating shots to a player according to his/her ability, allowing all standards of golfer to compete against each other on equal terms.

hanging lie When the ball comes to rest on a downslope.

hazards Bunkers or areas of water, say, on the course.

hole This is 4¼ inches (108 mm) in diameter and at least 4 inches (100 mm) deep.

hole in one An ace, ball hit into hole from tee.

holding A green is said to be holding when it is receptive to a shot and will 'hold' the ball on the putting surface; when a green is 'hard' it will reject the ball which will often bounce off the green.

honour On the 1st tee the player with the lowest handicap goes first and after that the player who has done best on the previous hole.

hook To hit the ball from right to left (for a right-hander).

jungle Slang for trees or bushes or any heavy rough.

lag To putt cautiously and avoid going well past the hole.

lay up To play short of a hazard in order to have the best position for the next shot.

lie Situation of the ball at rest. A 'good lie' would be a ball 'sitting up' well on the fairway.

line The direction you want to take with any given shot, as in 'the line you need to take off this tee is to aim at that big oak tree in the distance'; on the putting green it is the line to the hole, which will depend on the contours of the surface itself.

links Course built on sandy terrain, by the sea.

lip Rim of the hole, putts sometimes hit it and lip out.

local knowledge Advantage enjoyed by a player competing on a course they know well.

loose impediments Stones, twigs, leaves and other natural objects that get in the way of a ball being struck cleanly; can be removed without penalty but in so doing you must not move the ball; don't touch in hazards or bunkers.

lost ball A ball searched for and not found within the stipulated five minutes.

match play Contest decided on the winning of individual holes.

medal play Contest decided on the number of strokes taken to complete the course.

monthly medal The most common competition for members at most golf clubs, usually played on the same week of every month and split into handicap divisions.

mulligan An American illegality, taking a second shot off the first tee if the first one is no good.

muni/municipal course A course operated by the local authority for the general public.

nineteenth The first extra hole if sudden death is played in a match; also the clubhouse bar.

obstructions Man-made obstacles from which the golfer is entitled to relief without penalty.

out of bounds Anywhere beyond the defined limits of the golf course, often marked by white stakes; hitting a ball OB means a penalty.

par The base from which all scoring starts, the number of strokes allocated to a hole depending on its length, thus to par a hole, to be round in par and so on.

PGA Professional Golfers' Association, the body that nurtures golf outside the professional tour.

PGA European Tour The body that regulates and runs the professional tour.

pin Flagstick to show where the hole is on the green.

pitch Short shot, often hit high with a pitching wedge.

pitch mark Indentation made by a high, dropping ball on the putting surface and should be repaired as soon as the player gets to the green.

pivot The turning of the body in the swing.

play-off Extra hole, or holes, played to settle a tie.

plugged Ball embedded in sand, mud or wet grass.

pot bunker Small, steep-faced bunker, difficult to escape from.

pressing Attempting to hit the ball too hard, particularly when under pressure.

pro-am When a professional teams up with an amateur in competition; can also be a team event with three or even four amateurs partnering a professional and returning one score.

provisional ball Playing a second ball when it is suspected that the first might be lost or out of bounds.

pull To hit the ball well to the left (if you're right-handed).

push To hit the ball to the right (if you're right-handed).

putts per round The statistic that shows how many putts you have taken once the ball is actually on the green; using the putter from off the green does not count.

rabbit Novice, not a very good golfer.

range Can be the driving range, where you hit practice balls and take lessons, or can be the distance between you and the golfers in front – are they in or out of range.

rap A short, sharp putting stroke in which the putter stops the moment the ball is struck.

regulation To play a hole in par.

relief Taking a ball up and dropping it elsewhere, without penalty, under the rules.

rookie A player in his or her first year on a professional tour.

rough The long grass that borders and defines the fairways and punishes errant shots.

Royal and Ancient (R&A) The body that governs the game everywhere in the world bar the United States and Mexico.

rub of the green Golfing luck, good or bad.

run Distance the ball travels after landing.

Ryder Cup Biennial match between the top male professionals of Europe and the United States.

sand saves In simple terms to move from the sand of a greenside bunker to the bottom of the cup in two shots, or less; top professionals do this more than 80 per cent of the time.

scratch A scratch golfer is a player who has earned a handicap of nought (very good).

set A set of clubs, limited to 14 per player.

shank An inadvertent shot when the ball flies off almost at right angles after being hit by the neck of the club rather than the face.

shorty Slang for the player whose ball is the shortest off any given tee.

single A game between two players.

sky To hit the ball miles into the air, but not very far.

slice To move the ball sharply from left to right (for a right-hander).

Solheim Cup Biennial match between the top female professionals of Europe and the United States.

Stableford A system of playing golf for points, usually awarded as one for a bogey, two for a par, three for a birdie and so on.

stance Position of player before hitting the ball.

sticks Slang for your golf clubs.

stroke The act of intentionally hitting the ball (or trying to – also has to be counted even if the ball is missed).

stroke average The average number of strokes taken per round over a full season, usually on a professional tour.

stroke hole Where the player gives or receives a stroke under the handicapping system.

stroke play a round that is measured by the number of strokes taken.

sudden death See *play-off*.

sweet spot The area on the club face, in the middle, that produces the best strike; what every golfer on every shot is aiming to find.

takeaway The start of the swing.

tap in A very short putt, usually regarded as unmissable.

tee The area from which a hole is started.

tee peg Object, either wooden or plastic on which the ball can be perched for tee shots only.

tempo Another word for rhythm, both vital in order to play well.

Texas wedge American slang for a putter when used from off the green.

through the green An expression in the rules defining all the course except the tees, hazards and greens.

tiddler Slang for a short putt.

tiger Not just Mr Woods, but any golfer of high ability.

topping To hit the top half of the ball and cause it to run along the ground.

tradesman's entrance When a putt slips into the hole from the back or side of it.

trap Bunker in America, usually flattish and not a deep pit.

trolley Specially made cart to carry your golf bag; you pull it along (although many are battery operated now); called a *trundler* in Australia.

turn Halfway round the course, you reach the turn after nine holes; can also refer to the turning of the body in the golf swing.

under As in one under, two under and so on, meaning the number of strokes a player is under par; its opposite is one over, two over, etc.

up and down Getting the ball into the hole in two strokes from off the green.

waggle Moving the club around at address, in order to feel comfortable, or to relieve tension.

water hazard Defined by yellow stakes, marking out any sea, lake, pond, river, ditch or other open water course, whether or not, oddly, containing water or not; a lateral water hazard is marked by red stakes.

winter rules Temporary rules which allow the ball to be lifted, cleaned and placed on the fairway to help protect the course and make play possible in the sort of adverse ground conditions that often prevail in the winter.

yips A dreaded, nervous affliction causing the sufferer to jerk uncontrollably at putts, dispatching them he or she knows not where.

taking it further

You're in for a lot of fun if you get hooked on golf and the joy is that you'll never stop learning. There are books to read (this book might have been finished a lot sooner if we hadn't kept dipping in to old favourites and new temptations), videos or DVDs to watch and games to play on gadgets like PlayStation 2, Xbox, GameCube, PC, PSP and PS2 (all double Dutch to us but manna from heaven for the technically adept).

There is also a great deal of help available these days for every level of golfer, from beginner to expert, for old and, particularly, young, on the internet sites of the game's leading bodies. The websites are full of pointers and advice about how to improve your game and where to go to achieve it. You will be amazed at the amount of help available: it is well worth logging on.

Take, for instance, the PGA's website www.pga.info. There is almost everything that an aspiring golfer could need to know, including the names, telephone numbers, postal and email addresses of the secretary of every region. To save you looking them up, they are listed below:

Scottish Region: Secretary Peter Lloyd. Tel: 01764 661840 Email: scotland.region@pga.org.uk Address: Kings Lodge, Gleneagles, Auchterarder, Perthshire PH3 1NE.

North Region: Jim Croxton. Tel: 01204 496137.
Email: north.region@pga.org.uk Address: No. 2 Cottage, Bolton Golf Club, Lostock Park, Chorley New Road, Bolton BL6 4AJ.

Midland Region: Jon Sewell. Tel: 01455 824393.
Email: midland.region@pga.org.uk Address: Forest Hill Golf Club, Markfield Lane, Botcheston, Leicester LE9 9FJ.

West Region: Ray Ellis. Tel: 01392 877657.
Email: west.region@pga.org.uk Address: Exeter Golf and Country Club, Topsham Road, Countess Wear, Exeter, Devon EX2 7AE.

East Region: John Smith. Tel: 01279 652070.
Email: east.region@pga.org.uk Address: Bishops Stortford Golf Club, Dunmow Road, Bishops Stortford, Hertfordshire CM23 5HP.

South Region: Peter Ward. Tel: 01483 224200.
Email: south.region@pga.org.uk Address: Clandon Regis Golf Club, Epsom Road, West Clandon, Guildford, Surrey GU4 7TT.

Irish Region: Michael McCumiskey. Tel: 00353 (0) 42932 1193.
Email: irish.region@pga.org.uk Address: Dundalk Golf Club, Blackrock, Dundalk, County Louth, Ireland.

Women Professional Golfers Association: Maureen Roberts. Tel: 01675 470333. Email: maureen.roberts@pga.org.uk Address: Centenary House, The Belfry, Sutton Coldfield, West Midlands B76 9PT.

There are more than 7,000 qualified members of the PGA and the comprehensive website includes everything you need to know to get started in golf and just how to locate those professionals.

The PGA also has www.pgapro.tv, which is a broadband channel with streaming video footage featuring interviews and tournament coverage and equipment reviews.

There are a goodly number of municipal courses, where anyone can pay and play, given a reasonable knowledge of how to hit the ball and how to behave on a golf course so that you are not holding up others. There is a National Association of Public Golf Courses, which has an informative website at www.napgc.org.uk/napgc which, among other things, lists all the courses available to you.

Other helpful organizations include:

www.englishgolfunion.org
www.englishladiesgolf.org
www.gui.ie (Golfing Union of Ireland)
www.ilgu.ie (Irish Ladies Golf Union)
www.lgu.org (Ladies Golf Union)
www.scottishgolfunion.org

www.slga.scottishgolf.com (Scottish Ladies Golf Association)

www.welshgolf.org

www.wlgu.org.uk (Welsh Ladies Golf Union)

www.randa.org (Royal and Ancient, St Andrews), also

www.opengolf.com

www.clubgolfscotland.com (Scotland's initiative to introduce juniors to golf)

www.congu.com/home.asp (handicapping body for Britain and Ireland)

www.golf-foundation.org (to promote golf particularly among the young and in schools)

www.thefirstteeireland.org (to promote youth development through golf)

www.britishgolfmuseum.co.uk (to find out more about how this most wonderful of games developed, and is developing)

www.northwickpark.com (near the new Wembley Stadium, features Playgolf's unique 'golf in an hour')

www.pga.com (PGA of America)

www.cpga.com (Canadian PGA)

www.pgae.com (PGA of Europe)

www.pga.org.au (PGA of Australia)

www.ausgolfmuseum.com (Australasian Golf Museum in Tasmania)

www.asianpga.com

www.congu.com (the Council of National Golf Unions whose duties include administrating handicaps for club golfers in Great Britain and Ireland)

The following are sites connected to our contributors and there are email addresses and telephone numbers for some of them too. The others can be contacted through the PGA.

Eddie Birchenough – Royal Lytham and St Annes; Tel: 01253 720094

Luther Blacklock–Woburn; www.explanar.com; Tel: 01908 626600

Nigel Blenkarne – www.crown-golf.co.uk, doc@crown-golf.co.uk and www.ymg-golf.com

Gillian Burrell – gburrell@eircom.net

Simon Dicksee – www.simondicksee.com; simon.dicksee @hotmail.com

Dr Kitrina Douglas – www.acrossthetamar.co.uk

Peter Evans – Royal Porthcawl; Tel: 01656 773702

Lawrence Farmer – Moor Park; Tel: 01923 774113

Peter Lane – Harpenden; Tel: 01582 767124

Maureen Madill – mogolf99@aol.com; Tel: 07768 476619

Lynn Marriott and Pia Nilsson – www.golf54.com, Tel: 001 602 482 8983

Dr Karl Morris – www.golf-brain.com and www.trained-brain.com

Ian D. Rae – ianrae59@hotmail.com

Derek Simpson – Dereksgolfpro@aol.com

Gillian Stewart – www.gillianstewart.com; golf@gillianstewart.com; Tel: 07801 930034

Keith Williams – Tel: 07802 364663

Reading about golf is a joy and we'd recommend anything by Peter Alliss, Bernard Darwin, Peter Dobereiner, John Jacobs, Henry Longhurst, Harvey Penick and P. G. Wodehouse. They are just some of our own favourites and the list below includes a few more, chosen more or less at random.

Allis Through The Looking Glass (Peter Alliss with Bob Ferrier, Cassell, 1963)

A Season in Dornoch (Lorne Rubinstein, Mainstream Publishing, 2003)

A Woman's Way to Better Golf (Peggy Kirk Bell with Jerry Claussen, 1966)

Beyond the Fairways (David and Patricia Davies, Collins Willow, 1999)

Better Golf – Definitely! (Jessie Valentine, Pelham Books, 1967)

Breaking 80: The Life and Times of Joe Carr (Dermot Gilleece, Poolbeg, 2002)

Emerald Gems (Laurence Casey Lambrecht, Lambrecht Photography, 2002)

Every Shot I Take (Davis Love III, Simon & Schuster, 1997)

Every Shot Must Have A Purpose (Pia Nilsson and Lynn Marriott with Ron Sirak, Gotham Books, 2005)

Faults and Fixes (David Leadbetter, Collins Willow, 1994)

Forgive us our press passes (Association of Golf Writers, Lennard Queen Anne Press, 2005)

Golf Annika's Way (Annika Sorenstam, with the editors of *Golf magazine*, Gotham Books, 2004)

Golf In My Gallowses (Angus Mac Vicar and Jock MacVicar, Hutchinson, 1983)

Golf – The Mind Factor (Darren Clarke and Dr Karl Morris, Hodder & Stoughton, 2005)

Golfing days (Phil Sheldon and Liz Kahn, Mitchell Beazley, 2004)

Harvey Penick's Little Red Book (Harvey Penick and Bud Shrake, Collins Willow, 1993)

Jack Nicklaus, My Story (Jack Nicklaus and Ken Bowden, Ebury Press, 1997)

John Jacobs' Impact on Golf (Laddie Lucas, Stanley Paul, 1987)

One Minute Golfer (Ken Blanchard, Harper Collins, 2005)

Only Golf Lesson You'll Ever Need (Hank Haney, Harper Collins, 1999)

Practical Golf (John Jacobs, Stanley Paul, 1972)

50 Greatest Golf Lessons of the Century (John Jacobs, Harper Resource, 2000)

50 Years of Golfing Wisdom (John Jacobs and Steve Newell, Collins Willow, 2005)

100 Tips For Lady Golfers (Kitrina Douglas, Harper Collins, 1993)

Simply Toogood (Des Tobin, Killaghy Publishing, 2003)

Thanks for the Game (Henry Cotton, Sedgwick & Jackson, 1980)

The Complete Encyclopedia of Golf (Derek Lawrenson, Carlton, 1999)

The Golf Bag Buddy (Bill Elliott, David & Charles, 2005)

The Golf Omnibus (P. G. Wodehouse, Barrie & Jenkins, 1973)

The Historical Dictionary of Golfing Terms (Peter Davies, Robson Books, 1993)

The Royal & Ancient Golfer's Handbook (ed. Renton Laidlaw, Macmillan, 2005)

The Shell International Encyclopedia of Golf (ed. Donald Steel and Peter Ryde, Ebury Press and Pelham Books, 1975)

The Short Game Bible (Dave Pelz, Aurum Press, 1999)

The Swing Factory (William Sieghart, Steve Gould and D. J. Wilkinson, Simon & Schuster, 1997)

Winning Golf For Women (Beverly Lewis, Collins Willow, 1993)

And there's much, much more. Good luck. Have a ball.

index